Crime Prevention and Security Management

Series Editor
Martin Gill, Perpetuity Research, Tunbridge Wells, UK

It is widely recognized that we live in an increasingly unsafe society, but the study of security and crime prevention has lagged behind in its importance on the political agenda and has not matched the level of public concern. This exciting new series aims to address these issues looking at topics such as crime control, policing, security, theft, workplace violence and crime, fear of crime, civil disorder, white collar crime and anti-social behaviour. International in perspective, providing critically and theoretically-informed work, and edited by a leading scholar in the field, this series will advance new understandings of crime prevention and security management.

Tymur Suslov

Rethinking Security

The Human Side of Risk Management

Tymur Suslov
Haslemere, UK

ISSN 2946-3513   ISSN 2946-3521 (electronic)
Crime Prevention and Security Management
ISBN 978-3-031-92067-7   ISBN 978-3-031-92068-4 (eBook)
https://doi.org/10.1007/978-3-031-92068-4

© The Editor(s) (if applicable) and The Author(s), under exclusive license to Springer Nature Switzerland AG 2025

This work is subject to copyright. All rights are solely and exclusively licensed by the Publisher, whether the whole or part of the material is concerned, specifically the rights of translation, reprinting, reuse of illustrations, recitation, broadcasting, reproduction on microfilms or in any other physical way, and transmission or information storage and retrieval, electronic adaptation, computer software, or by similar or dissimilar methodology now known or hereafter developed.
The use of general descriptive names, registered names, trademarks, service marks, etc. in this publication does not imply, even in the absence of a specific statement, that such names are exempt from the relevant protective laws and regulations and therefore free for general use.
The publisher, the authors and the editors are safe to assume that the advice and information in this book are believed to be true and accurate at the date of publication. Neither the publisher nor the authors or the editors give a warranty, expressed or implied, with respect to the material contained herein or for any errors or omissions that may have been made. The publisher remains neutral with regard to jurisdictional claims in published maps and institutional affiliations.

Cover illustration: © Melisa Hasan

This Palgrave Macmillan imprint is published by the registered company Springer Nature Switzerland AG
The registered company address is: Gewerbestrasse 11, 6330 Cham, Switzerland

If disposing of this product, please recycle the paper.

Editor Series Introduction

All good security approaches include a requirement to understand the threat being faced, therefore any book seeking to inform the theory and practice of risk assessments is likely to attract the interest of both security practitioners and academics. The subject of security risk is characterised by being broad; encompassing many dimensions; and is continuously evolving. The need for up-to-date research and new thinking is critical. This book, with its focus on a human-centric approach to security risk management is therefore both timely and important.

This book offers more than just a discussion of a distinct approach to human-centric risk, it also provides a scholarly discussion of the limitations of an emphasis on the technical, or at least the need to reconcile this perspective with human factors, as the author, Tymur Suslov notes: "Technical barriers are easily undone if human users circumvent them". The book assesses perspectives from a variety of different disciplines such as psychology, criminology, sociology, and risk communication. And this is undertaken not just as an academic exercise but with a view to guiding organisations on how to improve not just risk assessments but also training courses and organisational cultures.

Tymur Suslov discusses a wide range of human factors, "such as individual perceptions, collective behaviours, group identities, and psychological vulnerabilities", all of which (and more) need to be considered to optimise the effectiveness of security provision. His book looks at how "risk misjudgement" and "criminal opportunism" occur; how humans provide a weak link when misunderstood, one that is essential to understand and be countered for security to have a chance of being effective. For Suslov the focus on the human rather than the technical means that the common risk management approach to arrive at a predictable outcome is at variance with the real world.

His discussion of risk perception includes a focus on emotions, past experiences, and cultural influences; while risk communication includes a look at the impact of psychological, social, and cultural factors. There is a big emphasis on psychological theories, including cognitive and social psychology, and a whole chapter is devoted to profiling, described as "complex," where the merits are balanced by the ethical and privacy concerns. On that point the key characteristics which underpin unethical and illegal behaviour, namely narcissism, psychopathy, and Machiavellianism are discussed. A particularly interesting chapter, at least for this reader was Suslov's discussion of how the qualities that underpin effective human interaction, including trust and empathy, are used to manipulate security systems.

Suslov's discussion of a range of criminological theories and crime prevention frameworks, including Routine Activity Theory and Situational Crime Prevention is undertaken from a human centred approach noting that effective crime prevention is always based "on both human behavioural insights and environmental design." After all, "security risks are a result of human behaviour, rather than technological constraints," and given that "human error continues to be the primary factor in the occurrence of security breaches" education and awareness are key components of any informed response.

Once you have digested the excellent introduction to this book you will, I am sure, be lured into the various chapters with enthusiasm. This topic is an important one, and I have no doubt that scholars and practitioners alike will find this book a "must read."

April 2025   Martin Gill

Contents

1 Introduction to the Book … 1

Part I Security Risk

2 Risk and Uncertainty … 9
3 Risk Perception … 15
4 Risk Communication … 23

Part II Psychology

5 Psychological Theories in the Context of Security … 37
6 Profiling and the Psychological Characteristics of Criminals … 47
7 Social Engineering and Manipulation … 57

Part III Criminology

8 Criminal Behaviour … 67
9 Crime Prevention … 73

Part IV New Approach

10	Human-Centric Models and Behavioural Security	85
11	Security Education	95

Index 105

CHAPTER 1

Introduction to the Book

Abstract Contemporary security threats have become more sophisticated, outpacing traditional technology-based solutions. This chapter emphasises the need of including human aspects into security risk management, illustrating that technology alone cannot sufficiently defend against vulnerabilities caused by human error, bias, and manipulation. It proposes a human-centered strategy, pushing for multidisciplinary ideas from psychology, criminology, sociology, and risk communication to address these difficulties holistically. The book's main goal is to balance technical safeguards with an understanding of human dynamics, therefore increasing organisational resilience to cyberattacks, insider threats, and social engineering approaches. The book, divided into four sections, rigorously investigates how perceptions, cognitive biases, criminal motives, and effective risk communication tactics interact with real security solutions. It is aimed at professionals, scholars, and general readers and gives empirical methodologies and concepts for developing a proactive, psychologically informed security culture.

Keywords Human-centric security · Insider threats · Risk environment · Behavioural factors · Interdisciplinary approach

Context and Importance

Contemporary security risks have significantly increased in complexity, sophistication, and effect. Governments, organisations, and private individuals contend with a variety of challenges, including extensive cyberattacks, insider threats, and well planned social engineering tactics. Conventional security frameworks, mostly centred on technology, find it challenging to adapt to the changing risk environment. Intrusion detection systems, firewalls, and encrypted communications are vital; but they can be readily compromised by the human agents that implement or engage with them. A solitary act of human negligence can nullify millions invested in sophisticated security systems.

In light of these issues, an increasing volume of research and experience underscores the necessity for a human-centric approach to security risk management. This perspective posits that security should not be regarded solely as a technical issue; instead, it underscores the significance of human factors—such as individual perceptions, collective behaviours, group identities, and psychological vulnerabilities—in influencing security outcomes, potentially more so than the most recent software patches or hardware enhancements. By examining the underlying motives and biases that contribute to risk misjudgement, insider threat, and criminal opportunism, security professionals may formulate more effective and adaptable measures that address root causes.

Principal Themes and Objectives

The fundamental objective of this book is to reconcile technological and human factors, enabling readers to see why technology alone cannot adequately protect important assets or information. Technical barriers are easily undone if human users circumvent them. Cybercriminals can exploit psychological weaknesses much faster than organisations can update or patch hardware and software. Thus, a security programme that neglects human dynamics is susceptible to vulnerabilities.

The book employs an interdisciplinary approach, integrating studies from psychology, criminology, sociology, and risk communication to tackle these challenges. Every chapter utilises lessons from various disciplines to elucidate the intangible yet essential human aspects of security. The book emphasises practical consequences for policymakers, business leaders, IT workers, and others tasked with managing security risks. Readers will find empirical techniques to enhance training programmes, risk evaluations, criminal deterrence strategies, and overall organisational cultures.

Framework of the Book's Composition

The book comprises 11 chapters, organised into four principal sections. Each section emphasises distinct aspects of human-centric security, leading the reader from fundamental risk ideas to innovative, collaborative security frameworks.

Part 1. Security Risk

Chapter 2: Uncertainty and Risk

This chapter delineates security risk and advocates for a human-centred perspective that considers behaviour, perception, and uncertainty. It challenges conventional, technology-centric paradigms and creates a foundation for the subsequent, more nuanced evaluations.

Chapter 3: Risk Perception

Risk is subjective, influenced by biases, emotions, and cultural factors. Chapter 3 explores the psychological foundations of individuals' evaluations and responses to dangers, frequently diverging from expert analyses. The chapter highlights how skewed risk perception can impede the implementation of logical, evidence-based security solutions into secure behaviours.

Chapter 4: Risk Communication

Reconciling public and organisational perceptions with actual risks constitutes a fundamental problem. Chapter 4 examines fundamental ideas of risk communication, elucidating how clarity in messaging, trust, and credibility promote significant participation. It attacks the "information deficit model" in favour of methodologies that prioritise discussion, framing strategies, and the influence of technology in the dissemination (or distortion) of risk signals.

Section 1.2: Psychology

Chapter 5: Psychological Theories in the Context of Security

Cognitive biases, emotional conditions, and social influences significantly affect security results for both perpetrators and protectors. This chapter analyses how cognitive load, groupthink, and motivational variables can undermine well-structured security regulations, emphasising the necessity of psychological insight in forecasting and regulating security-related behaviours.

Chapter 6: Profiling and Psychological Characteristics of Criminals

Certain psychological characteristics—namely narcissism, psychopathy, and Machiavellianism—frequently manifest in persons who perpetrate security breaches. Chapter 6 examines these characteristics, illustrating how profiling might assist in identifying possible dangers. By comprehending the characteristics and motives of attackers, organisations may create more tailored and proactive security strategies.

Chapter 7: Social Engineering and Manipulation

The emphasis here is on how adversaries methodically exploit human vulnerabilities to circumvent technology protections. This chapter illustrates that social engineering, encompassing cognitive biases, emotional appeals, and social influence strategies, is a significant threat to security integrity. Comprehending these strategies is crucial for developing defences that target human, as opposed to solely technological, weaknesses.

Section 1.3: Criminology

Chapter 8: Criminal Behaviour

This chapter examines fundamental criminological ideas, including Routine Activity Theory, Rational Choice Theory, and Strain Theory, in relation to insider threats, cyberattacks, and organised crime. Analysing the environmental and situational catalysts that promote criminal behaviour provides readers with an understanding of the systematic foundations of seeming haphazard security violations.

Chapter 9: Crime Prevention

Effective crime prevention techniques are established by proactive interventions that reduce both opportunities and incentives. Chapter 9 presents techniques like Situational Crime Prevention, Crime Prevention Through Environmental Design (CPTED), and Behaviour Change frameworks, demonstrating how these strategies prevent criminal actions prior to their occurrence.

Section 1.4: Innovative Methodology

Chapter 10: Behavioural Security

Conventional "command and control" frameworks frequently foster compliance-oriented attitudes instead of authentic security culture. Chapter 10 advocates for a collaborative and adaptable framework that unites many departments, utilises public–private partnerships, and promotes international collaboration. This transition towards behavioural security acknowledges that contemporary dangers surpass organisational and governmental limits.

Chapter 11: Security Education and Psychological Resilience

Chapter 11 contends that security education should transition from outdated, mechanical compliance training to engaging, psychology-based programmes that promote enduring behavioural transformation. It elucidates how emotional and cognitive engagement, memory retention techniques, and resilience-enhancing practices may transform the responses of people and organisations to challenges. The book emphasises that practical guidance on gamification, scenario-based learning, and interdepartmental collaboration highlights a core theme: the significance of the human element is crucial, and robust security relies on the successful education and empowerment of individuals.

Target Audience

This book will serve several professional and academic communities:

Security professionals and policymakers, including CISOs, security managers, and government agencies, will discover methodologies for incorporating psychological and criminological insights into routine operations. By including the human factor in risk assessment and using adaptive, human-centric crime prevention strategies, they may enhance defences against evolving threats.

Academic and Research Communities: Scholars and students in cybersecurity, psychology, criminology, and risk management can enhance their comprehension of the multidisciplinary aspects of security. The book's citations of empirical evidence and theoretical constructs render it pertinent for advanced scholarship and research partnerships.

General Readers Interested in Security: The subjects addressed—spanning social engineering to insider threat analysis—are articulated in comprehensible language, supported by practical examples. Those interested in the intersection of contemporary security issues and human behaviour will acquire understanding of the concepts influencing daily security choices.

Methodological and Theoretical Foundations

This book utilises an interdisciplinary amalgamation of scholarly literature, case studies, and theoretical frameworks:

Psychological and Behavioural Research: Insights from cognitive, social, and affective psychology clarify the reasons individuals miscalculate risks, fall prey to social engineering, or engage in security violations.

Criminological Paradigms: The amalgamation of Routine Activity Theory, Rational Choice Theory, and Strain Theory provides systematic methods for identifying the fundamental causes of crime and forecasting criminal behaviour.

Studies on Risk Communication: Utilising insights from risk perception and communication research, the paper delineates strategies to enhance message clarity, credibility, and trust—essential elements for any security awareness initiative.

Case Analyses with Empirical Data: Chapters, where applicable, cite actual events (e.g., significant cyber breaches, whistleblower situations) to illustrate the manifestation of theoretical ideas in practical circumstances.

The analysis seeks to harmonise theoretical discourse with practical advice, enabling readers to use the concepts inside actual security environments.

Conclusion

In a landscape characterised by sophisticated hacking tools, financially robust criminal organisations, and state-sponsored espionage, an exclusive emphasis on technology is inadequate. The human element—encompassing its intricacies, biases, and motivating forces—constitutes both the most significant risk and the most formidable advantage in security. This book presents a comprehensive, adaptable, and human-centred perspective on security by examining how individuals perceive and communicate dangers, engage in criminal behaviour, and collaborate to foster resilience.

PART I

Security Risk

CHAPTER 2

Risk and Uncertainty

Abstract Uncertainty is a fundamental component of security risk, resulting from inherent randomness (aleatory uncertainty) and incomplete information (epistemic uncertainty). Behavioural research underscores the impact of cognitive biases, including overconfidence and heuristics, on risk perception, despite the fact that traditional risk management models rely on statistical analysis. Furthermore, Douglas and Wildavsky's cultural theory of risk posits that risk is influenced by social and cultural constructs. In this chapter, the intricacies of uncertainty in security contexts are examined, with a focus on the constraints of deterministic models and the promotion of adaptive risk management strategies.

Keywords Aleatory and epistemic uncertainty · Cognitive biases · Behavioural risk perception · Adaptive risk management · Social construction of risk

Introduction

Particularly in the realm of security risk management, where hazards are frequently unpredictable and intricate, uncertainty is an inherent component of decision-making. Uncertainty is the absence of complete knowledge regarding future events or outcomes, which affects the assessment and response to hazards of individuals, organisations, and governments. Security risk encompasses both aleatory uncertainty, which is predicated on inherent randomisation, and epistemic uncertainty, which is derived from incomplete information.

Statistical models are employed by conventional risk management frameworks to quantify threats and devise mitigation strategies. Nevertheless, behavioural research indicates that cognitive biases, including overconfidence and heuristics, can influence risk perception, resulting in misguided security decisions sometimes. Furthermore, risk is a social construct that is influenced by institutional narratives and cultural values.

This chapter investigates the nature of uncertainty in security contexts, analysing both quantitative and qualitative risk assessment methods. Organisations can improve their resilience in a changing security environment by incorporating continuous monitoring and adaptive strategies.

In its broadest sense, uncertainty is the condition of possessing inadequate knowledge regarding future events, outcomes, or fundamental conditions (Rakow, 2010).

This distinction is the foundation of a significant portion of the economic, psychological, and philosophical discourse regarding the responses of individuals and societies to ambiguous situations. The core of human existence is uncertainty, whether it pertains to daily decisions, such as selecting a new employment, or societal challenges, such as managing emerging technologies.

Numerous cognitive mechanisms have been devised by humans to manage uncertainty from a psychological perspective. These strategies encompass a wide variety of approaches, including straightforward heuristics for rapid decision-making and intricate scenario planning models. Cognitive bias is a fundamental response, as demonstrated by the research of Tversky and Kahneman (1974). They demonstrated that individuals rely on mental heuristics, such as availability and representativeness, to evaluate probabilities in the presence of uncertainty. While these shortcuts frequently facilitate the rapidity of decision-making, they may also result in systematic errors or overconfident judgements. In these circumstances, the wish for a straightforward, predictable outcome is at odds with the inherent ambiguity of real-world events.

Uncertainty can elicit emotional responses that range from mild anxiety to severe distress (Grupe & Nitschke, 2013). In general, humans prefer environments that are stable and predictable, as the brain's threat detection systems are activated by unpredictability. Diverse strategies are implemented by individuals to manage uncertainty on an individual basis. Information-seeking is one approach, in which individuals endeavour to mitigate ambiguity by acquiring additional data or consulting with experts (Mousavi & Gigerenzer, 2014).

Security risk is fundamentally characterised by uncertainty. Epistemic uncertainty, which is the absence of comprehensive knowledge regarding prospective threats and vulnerabilities, is one of the primary obstacles to security risk management (Hüllermeier & Waegeman, 2021). This is especially apparent in zero-day vulnerabilities, which are undetected until they are exploited. Hüllermeier and Waegeman (2021) define aleatory uncertainty as the inherent randomness, which is another form of uncertainty. For instance, the probability of a particular organisation being the target of a cyberattack is contingent upon external factors that are beyond its control, such as geopolitical tensions or changing criminal motivations.

Security risk is a multifaceted concept that transcends the technical domain and encompasses the social, psychological, and organisational spheres. Security risk is typically defined as the sum of the potential severity of the consequences of a security violation and the likelihood of its occurrence. The estimation of risk in conventional risk management models is based on statistical and actuarial methodologies, which presuppose that hazards can be predicted, controlled, and mitigated through systematic analysis. ISO 31000:2018 defines risk as the "effect of uncertainty on objectives," emphasising its intrinsically uncertain and dynamic nature.

Nevertheless, security risk is not solely quantitative or objective; it is also subject to contextual interpretations, cognitive biases, and human perception (Aven, 2016). Contemporary scholarship acknowledges that risk is not a solitary objective reality, but rather a socially constructed phenomenon that fluctuates across various contexts (Wong, 2018).

Statistical techniques are assumed to be capable of identifying, measuring, and mitigating risks in conventional risk management frameworks, such as those founded on probability theory (Aven, 2016).

However, the application of deterministic or probabilistic models with certainty is often challenging due to the unpredictable nature of security threats (Taleb, 2007).

Traditional risk matrices, heat maps, and probabilistic models frequently fail to provide precise risk assessments in light of these uncertainties. Rather, security professionals are increasingly implementing adaptive risk management strategies that include machine learning-driven anomaly detection, real-time threat intelligence, and continuous monitoring (Mahboubi et al., 2024). These methods recognise that security hazards cannot always be predicted and must be managed dynamically.

However, research in behavioural security indicates that risk perceptions vary significantly among individuals and organisations, contrary to the assumption that actors make rational security decisions based on empirical data in traditional risk models. The assessment and prioritisation of threats are significantly influenced by factors such as media influence, prior experiences, and institutional biases (Bambals, 2015).

Environmental and systemic variables are also significant factors in security risk. Complexity theory posits that security risks arise in interdependent systems, where minor disruptions can escalate into significant crises. This is especially pertinent in the context of global supply chains and cybersecurity, where minor vulnerabilities can result in cascading failures. Consequently, risk management must consider emergent threats, adaptive adversaries, and non-linear interactions, rather than restricting itself to historical data and probability models (Johnson & Covello, 1987).

Security risk is increasingly acknowledged as a socially constructed phenomenon, in addition to its statistical and predictive dimensions. According to social constructivist perspectives, risk is not an inherent characteristic of hazards, but rather a result of collective beliefs, cultural values, and institutional narratives. Different societies, organisations, and individuals perceive and respond to risk in unique ways, which are influenced by historical experiences, political ideologies, and social conditioning (Karacasulu & Uzgören, 2007).

Douglas and Wildavsky (1982) devised the cultural theory of risk, which further elucidates the reasons why different groups perceive security hazards in different ways. This theory posits that risk perception is influenced by institutional norms, group identity, and social structures.

Quantitative risk models are inadequate for comprehending security risk, which is a multifaceted and constantly changing concept. Although conventional definitions prioritise threat probabilities and potential consequences, an expanding corpus of research underscores the social and psychological aspects of risk perception. Risk is a dynamic construct that is influenced by cultural, institutional, and political contexts, rather than a static entity. The notion of risk as an objective phenomenon is challenged by the comprehension of security risk as a social construct, which promotes more adaptive, context-sensitive approaches to security risk management.

Conclusion

Security risk is inherently characterised by uncertainty, which influences decision-making at the individual, organisational, and systemic levels. Traditional risk management models presuppose that statistical analyses can be used to predict and mitigate threats. However, real-world security risks frequently arise unexpectedly as a result of epistemic and aleatory uncertainties. Cognitive fallacies, including overconfidence and heuristics, exacerbate the complexity of risk assessment, resulting in inaccurate security strategy decisions.

In addition to probabilistic models, social and cultural factors also influence security risk. The cultural theory of risk developed by Douglas and Wildavsky emphasises the impact of societal structures and institutional narratives on the perception of threats. Adaptive risk management strategies—which incorporate real-time intelligence and continuous monitoring—are indispensable for managing dynamic risks as security landscapes change. The recognition of risk as a socially constructed phenomenon facilitates a more adaptable, context-sensitive security approach, thereby increasing resilience to emergent threats.

References

Aven, T. (2016). Risk assessment and risk management: Review of recent advances on their foundation. *European Journal of Operational Research, 253*(1), 1–13.

Bambals, R. (2015). Human security: An analytical tool for disaster perception research. *Disaster Prevention and Management, 24*(2), 150–165.

Douglas, M., & Wildavsky, A. (1982). *Risk and culture: An essay on the selection of technological and environmental dangers* (1st ed.). University of California Press.

Grupe, D. W., & Nitschke, J. B. (2013). Uncertainty and anticipation in anxiety: An integrated neurobiological and psychological perspective. *Nature Reviews Neuroscience, 14*(7), 488–501.

Hüllermeier, E., & Waegeman, W. (2021). Aleatoric and epistemic uncertainty in machine learning: An introduction to concepts and methods. *Machine Learning, 110*, 457–506.

ISO (2018). ISO 31000 : 2018, Risk management - guidelines. Vernier, Geneva International Organization For Standardization.

Johnson, B. B., & Covello, V. T. (1987). *The social and cultural construction of risk: Essays on risk selection and perception.* D. Reidel Publishing Company.

Karacasulu, N., & Uzgören, E. (2007). Explaining social constructivist contributions to security studies. *Perceptions: Journal of International Affairs, 12*(3), 27–48.

Mahboubi, A., Luong, K., Aboutorab, H., Bui, H. T., Jarrad, G., Bahutair, M., & Gately, H. (2024) Evolving techniques in cyber threat hunting: A systematic review. *Journal of Network and Computer Applications*, 104004.

Mousavi, S., & Gigerenzer, G. (2014). Risk, uncertainty, and heuristics. *Journal of Business Research, 67*(8), 1671–1678.

Rakow, T. (2010). Risk, uncertainty and prophet: The psychological insights of Frank H. *Knight, Judgment and Decision Making, 5*(6), 458–466.

Taleb, N. N. (2007). *The Black Swan.* Random House.

Tversky, A., & Kahneman, D. (1974) Judgment under Uncertainty: Heuristics and Biases: Biases in judgments reveal some heuristics of thinking under uncertainty. *Science, 185*(4157), 1124–1131.

Wong, C. M. L. (2018). Risk in social theory. In *Energy, risk and governance.* Palgrave Macmillan.

CHAPTER 3

Risk Perception

Abstract Risk perception is the subjective evaluation of potential hazards, which is influenced by cognitive biases, emotive responses, social influences, and cultural factors. Although security professionals depend on data-driven risk analysis, individuals frequently interpret risks using heuristics, such as optimism bias or availability bias, which can result in inaccurate assessments. Public perceptions are further amplified or distorted by media narratives and digital platforms, which in turn influence collective risk behaviours. This chapter investigates the psychological and social mechanisms that underlie risk perception, emphasising the influence of personal experiences, demographic factors, and societal norms on security-related decision-making practices. In order to improve security preparedness, it is essential to comprehend these dynamics in order to develop effective risk communication strategies and align public perceptions with actual risks.

Keywords Subjective evaluations · Heuristics and biases · Influence of media · Emotional factors · Cultural and social contexts

Introduction

Risk perception is the subjective assessment of potential hazards, which is influenced by cognitive processes, emotions, past experiences, and social contexts. Although objective risk assessments are based on empirical data and probabilities, individuals frequently perceive risks that are influenced by personal biases, heuristics, and media exposure. Understanding these psychological mechanisms is indispensable for risk communication and security management.

Cognitive fallacies, including the optimism bias and the availability heuristic, influence individuals' risk assessments. Emotional states, such as anxiety and overconfidence, can further influence risk evaluations, resulting in exaggerated or underestimated threats. Furthermore, the prioritisation of risks by various populations is influenced by cultural and social factors, which in turn affects collective security responses.

The public's perception of risk is significantly influenced by media and digital platforms. Sensationalised coverage and misinformation can exacerbate or distort security concerns, resulting in misalignments between perceived and actual risks. This chapter delves into the psychological, social, and cultural aspects of risk perception, emphasising its implications for the development of security policies and decision-making.

Sensory transduction is the initial step in the process of perception, during which external stimuli—such as light waves, sound vibrations, and chemical signals—are transformed into neural impulses (Kandel et al., 2012). These stimuli are detected by specialised receptor cells in the epidermis, nostrils, eyes, and tongue, which transmit electrical signals to the central nervous system via neural pathways (Mesulam, 1998). For instance, photoreceptors in the visual system are activated by particles that strike the retina, which enable them to distinguish between wavelengths, intensities, and patterns. This initial phase is occasionally referred to as "low-level processing" due to its focus on fundamental attributes, including colour contrast and luminosity (Binder et al., 2017).

However, even at this stage, selective attention can influence the information that is ultimately detected: individuals may prioritise certain stimuli or filter out others based on their motivational states or tasks (Jimenez et al., 2020; Stevens & Bavelier, 2012). The brain begins to interpret and integrate rudimentary features into meaningful representations after encoding them in various cortical areas, particularly in the occipital, temporal, and parietal lobes. This phenomenon is referred to as "high-level" or "mid-level" processing, which involves the interpretation of contextual information, spatial orientation, and object recognition (Peirce, 2015). The brain is capable of identifying objects, locations, and faces by comparing incoming sensory data with stored templates or experiences. Nevertheless, this matching process is not merely an automated database search. When sensory input is incomplete or ambiguous, neural mechanisms make inferences, fill in voids, and even embellish raw data (Freeman & Ambady, 2011). As a result, perception is contingent upon both real-time sensory inputs and stored representations that have been influenced by learning and prior exposure.

The brain attributes meaning and significance to these synthesised representations, which is the culmination of cognitive interpretation. This process is dependent on networks that involve the prefrontal cortex, where executive functions such as impulse control and decision-making converge with perceptual data (Kandel et al., 2012). Therefore, perception is inextricably linked to action: the way in which an individual perceives their environment can elicit specific responses, ranging from basic reflexes to intricate social or defensive behaviours.

Despite the fact that biology establishes the fundamental architecture for perception, the interpretation of the continuous stream of sensory information is influenced by past experiences, emotions, and cognitive biases. Cognitive biases, such as confirmation bias or availability heuristics, can cause individuals to selectively observe data that is consistent with their expectations or recent memories, thereby potentially distorting the objective assessment of real-world conditions (Tversky & Kahneman, 1974). The perception is similarly distorted by emotional states. Fear can increase vigilance towards potential hazards, causing an individual to be hyper-alert to perceived threats while potentially disregarding benign features of the environment (Loewenstein et al., 2001). Conversely, complacency or overconfidence can suppress caution, resulting in the disregard of valid warning signals or the adoption of risk-taking behaviour.

The interpretation of new stimuli is significantly influenced by antecedent experiences, which in turn determine perception (Snyder et al., 2015). An individual's interpretive framework is influenced by their past successes, traumas, and learnt associations. This phenomenon elucidates the reasons why hazards are perceived differently by individuals from varying backgrounds.

It is clear that perception is never a direct reflection of external reality, given the multifaceted nature of sensory processing, memory integration, and affective modulation. Rather, it is generated through active reconstruction, a process that entails the development of narratives, interpretive frameworks, and selective attention (Freeman & Ambady, 2011). This reconstruction is context-dependent, which means that the characteristics of a situation that are highlighted and evaluated are influenced by a variety of factors, including the social setting, cultural background, time constraints, and personal stakes in the outcome. The mind's ability to be deceived by context or prior assumptions is illustrated by phenomena such as optical illusions and ambiguous stimuli, which illustrate the divergence between subjective perception and objective conditions (Carbon, 2014; Tyler, 2022).

Perception is also significantly influenced by social and cultural factors. Research in cultural psychology has demonstrated that the world is perceived differently by individuals from varying cultural backgrounds. Nisbett and Masuda (2003) discovered that individuals from Western, individualistic societies are more inclined to concentrate on focal objects in a scene, whereas those from Eastern, collectivist cultures are more inclined to pay attention to contextual relationships and peripheral details. These distinctions are indicative of cognitive approaches that are deeply rooted in culture and that affect a wide range of activities, including risk assessment and decision-making.

In the context of security, risk perception is a critical factor in the development of both individual and collective behaviours. The manner in which individuals perceive security concerns has a direct impact on their attitudes, behaviours, and decision-making processes regarding safety. Nevertheless, risk perception is not an objective concept; it is influenced by a multitude of factors, such as the interaction between security professionals and the public, individual characteristics, social and cultural contexts, and media portrayals. It is imperative to comprehend the manner in which these factors influence the perception of security risks in order to facilitate the development of security policies and effective risk communication.

Psychological and demographic factors, including age, gender, experience, and personality characteristics, can contribute to differences in risk perception among individuals. In certain domains, aged individuals frequently perceive hazards as more severe than their younger counterparts, according to research (Nolte & Hanoch, 2023; Bohem et al., 2015). Perceived security risk is also influenced by gender. Research suggests that women generally regard security hazards as more significant than men (Logan & Walker, 2017; Stevens et al., 2020). Furthermore, an individual's prior experiences with security vulnerabilities or criminality can increase their awareness of pertinent warning signals, resulting in a more cautious approach to risks than an individual without such a history (Ohman, 2017).

Security risk perception is a socially constructed phenomenon that is influenced by societal values and cultural norms, in addition to being an individual cognitive process. Sociologists and anthropologists who specialise in risk have noted that cultural values have a significant impact on judgements, resulting in various groups prioritising specific hazards over others (Douglas & Wildavsky, 1982).

The public's perceptions of security hazards are substantially influenced by media, which encompasses both traditional news outlets and digital platforms. The Social Amplification of Risk Framework (SARF) offers a theoretical foundation for comprehending the extent to which media coverage enhances or diminishes risk perception (Kasperson et al., 2022). The framing, frequency, and emotional tone of media coverage can either amplify or diminish risks, as per the Social Amplification of Risk Framework (SARF). For instance, the public tends to overestimate the probability of high-profile terrorist attacks due to the widespread media attention they receive. Conversely, cyber threats that are more pervasive but less dramatic, such as data breaches or phishing, receive limited coverage despite their higher probability.

The perception of security risk is further distorted by fear-based messaging in media and social networks (Garfin et al., 2022). Research indicates that the framing of security threats in a negative perspective (e.g., emphasising potential consequences rather than preventive measures) leads to an increase in public anxiety and defensive behaviours (Garzia et al., 2021). Cinelli et al. (2021) and Figa and Arfini (2022) have demonstrated that social media platforms exacerbate risk perception biases by promoting algorithm-driven content that reinforces pre-existing concerns. The rapid dissemination of security-related rumours on platforms like Twitter and Facebook demonstrates how digital media can exacerbate risk concerns beyond objective threat levels.

The perception of risk by security professionals and the general public is significantly different, and this discrepancy has significant implications for security policy and risk communication. Security professionals, including law enforcement officers, cybersecurity experts, and emergency responders, frequently evaluate risks using empirical data, statistical analyses, and expert knowledge. Security professionals typically acquire a more sophisticated comprehension of risks as a result of their specialised training and exposure to systematic risk assessment methodologies. In contrast, the general public frequently employs emotional reactions, personal experiences, and media portrayals to evaluate security risks, which can result in potential misalignments between perceived and actual threats. This discrepancy in risk perception can lead to an overestimation of more prevalent risks, such as cybercrime or health-related risks, and an overabundance of concern regarding specific risks (e.g., terrorism or violent crime). Security professionals must recognise the social and psychological factors that influence public perception and integrate these insights into risk communication strategies to improve their efficacy.

Conclusion

Cognitive fallacies, emotions, past experiences, and cultural influences all contribute to the intricate psychological and social process of risk perception. Although sensory processing is the bedrock of perception, individuals' risk assessments are influenced by higher-order cognitive mechanisms, including biases and heuristics. Decision-making can be influenced by psychological factors such as confirmation bias and optimism bias, which can result in an overestimation or underestimation of security hazards.

The perception and prioritisation of hazards are further influenced by social and cultural contexts. Variations in security risk perception are influenced by individual experiences, demographic factors, and societal values. Furthermore, media and digital platforms have a substantial impact on public attitudes and behaviours by either exacerbating or underplaying security threats.

It is imperative to comprehend the discrepancy between the public's and experts' perceptions of risk in order to enhance security strategies and risk communication. Security professionals can ensure that public concerns are in alignment with actual threats by incorporating psychological insights and effective communication methods. This gap can be bridged. A more resilient security culture is cultivated, preparedness is improved, and informed decision-making is promoted through a nuanced approach to risk perception.

References

Binder, M., Gociewicz, K., Windey, B., Koculak, M., Finc, K., Nikadon, J., Derda, M., & Cleeremans, A. (2017). The levels of perceptual processing and the neural correlates of increasing subjective visibility. *Consciousness and Cognition, 55*, 106–125.

Bonem, E. M., Ellsworth, P. C., & Gonzalez, R. (2015). Age differences in risk: Perceptions, intentions and domains. *Journal of Behavioral Decision Making, 28*(4), 317–330.

Carbon, C. C. (2014) Understanding human perception by human-made illusions. *Frontiers in Human Neuroscience, 8*(566).

Cinelli, M., Morales, G. D. F., Galeazzi, A., Quattrociocchi, W., & Starnini, M. (2021). The echo chamber effect on social media. *Proceedings of the National Academy of Sciences, 118*(9), 1–8.

Douglas, M., & Wildavsky, A. (1982). *Risk and culture : An essay on the selection of technological and environmental dangers.* University of California Press.

Figà Talamanca, G., & Arfini, S. (2022) Through the newsfeed glass: Rethinking filter bubbles and echo chambers. *Philosophy & Technology, 35*(1).

Freeman, J. B., & Ambady, N. (2011). A dynamic interactive theory of person construal. *Psychological Review, 118*(2), 247–279.

Garfin, D. R., Holman, E. A., Fischhoff, B., Wong-Parodi, G., & Silver, R. C. (2022). Media exposure, risk perceptions, and fear: Americans' behavioral responses to the Ebola public health crisis. *International Journal of Disaster Risk Reduction, 77*, Article 103059.

Garzia, F., Borghini, F., Mino, L., Bruni, A., Ramalingam, S., & Lombardi, M. (2021) *Emotional reactions to risk perception in the Herculaneum Archaeological Park* (pp. 1–6). University of Hertfordshire Research Archive (University of Hertfordshire).

Jimenez, M., Hinojosa, J. A., & Montoro, P. R. (2020). Visual awareness and the levels of processing hypothesis: A critical review. *Consciousness and Cognition, 85*, Article 103022.

Kandel, E. R., Schwartz, J. H., Jessell, T. M., Siegelbaum, S. A., Hudspeth, A. J., & Mack, S. (2012). *Principles of neural science* (5th edn.). McGraw-Hill Education.

Kasperson, R. E., Webler, T., Ram, B., & Sutton, J. (2022). The social amplification of risk framework: New perspectives. *Risk Analysis, 42*(7), 1367–1380.

Loewenstein, G. F., Weber, E. U., Hsee, C. K., & Welch, N. (2001). Risk as feelings. *Psychological Bulletin, 127*(2), 267–286.

Logan, T., & Walker, R. (2017). The gender safety gap: Examining the impact of victimization history, perceived risk, and personal control. *Journal of Interpersonal Violence, 36*(1–2), 088626051772940.

Mesulam, M. (1998). From sensation to cognition. *Brain, 121*(6), 1013–1052.

Nisbett, R. E., & Masuda, T. (2003). Culture and point of view. *Proceedings of the National Academy of Sciences*, *100*(19), 11163–11170.

Nolte, J., & Hanoch, Y. (2023). Adult age differences in risk perception and risk taking. *Current Opinion in Psychology*, *55*, Article 101746.

Ohman, S. (2017). Previous experiences and risk perception: The role of transference. *Journal of Education, Society and Behavioural Science*, *23*(1), 1–10.

Peirce, J. W. (2015). Understanding mid-level representations in visual processing. *Journal of Vision*, *15*(7), 5.

Snyder, J. S., Schwiedrzik, C. M., Vitela, A. D., & Melloni, L. (2015) How previous experience shapes perception in different sensory modalities. *Frontiers in Human Neuroscience*, *9*.

Stevens, C., & Bavelier, D. (2012). The role of selective attention on academic foundations: A cognitive neuroscience perspective. *Developmental Cognitive Neuroscience*, *2*(1), S30–S48.

Stevens, D., Bulmer, S., Banducci, S., & Vaughan-Williams, N. (2020). Male warriors and worried women? Understanding gender and perceptions of security threats. *European Journal of International Security*, *6*(1), 44–65.

Tversky, A., & Kahneman, D. (1974). Judgment under Uncertainty: Heuristics and Biases: Biases in judgments reveal some heuristics of thinking under uncertainty. *Science*, *185*(4157), 1124–1131.

Tyler, C. W. (2022). The nature of illusions: A new synthesis based on verifiability. *Frontiers in Human Neuroscience*, *16*, Article 875829.

CHAPTER 4

Risk Communication

Abstract Risk communication is an essential component of security management, as it affects the way in which individuals and organisations perceive and respond to threats. This chapter investigates the transition of risk communication from a one-way dissemination paradigm to an interactive, engagement-driven approach. It examines critical theoretical frameworks, such as the Information Deficit Model, the Mental Models Approach, and the Cultural Cognition Framework, which elucidate the manner in which cognitive, social, and cultural factors influence risk perceptions. The chapter also discusses the influence of media and technology on risk narratives, underscoring the necessity of communication strategies that are inclusive, transparent, and trustworthy. Public trust is improved, security preparedness is promoted, and vulnerabilities are mitigated in an ever-evolving threat landscape through the implementation of effective risk communication.

INTRODUCTION

Risk communication is a critical element of security management, as it enables individuals and organisations to effectively comprehend and respond to potential hazards. It is not merely a matter of disseminating information; it is a strategic process that entails the engagement of stakeholders, the resolution of concerns, and the cultivation of trust to guarantee that risk mitigation behaviours are implemented. The alignment of public perception with actual risk is essential for effective decision-making in areas such as cybersecurity, public health, and emergency response, where risk communication plays a critical role.

In the past, risk communication was perceived as a one-way process in which experts communicated information to the public. Nevertheless, modern methodologies prioritise reciprocal communication, acknowledging that cognitive biases, social influences, and cultural contexts influence public perceptions. Theories such as the Information Deficit Model, the Mental Models Approach, and the Cultural Cognition Framework underscore the importance of customised messaging strategies and the complex nature of risk perception.

The proliferation of digital communication and social media has revolutionised the communicated and received of risk messages, presenting both opportunities and challenges. Although these platforms facilitate the rapid dissemination of information, they also contribute to polarisation and misinformation. This chapter delves into the psychological, social, and technological aspects of risk communication, with a particular focus on the development of strategies that will improve public trust, engagement, and security preparedness.

In general, risk communication is defined as the interactive process of sharing information about hazards—whether related to public health, environmental threats, or security incidents—with stakeholders who may be affected or have a vested interest (Fischhoff, 1995). It has been defined in various ways. It is distinct from the mere dissemination of data in that it involves a conscious endeavour to customise messages to the preferences of the audience, promote dialogue, and promote mutual comprehension. Risk communication has historically been a response to public controversies regarding scientific and technological issues, such as nuclear power or chemical hazards. It has since expanded to encompass a wider range of topics, including terrorism threats, cyber risks, and pandemic response (Slovic, 2000).

It is essential for the alignment of public perceptions with evidence-based risk assessments, the promotion of appropriate security behaviours, and the cultivation of trust in risk management initiatives. In the past, risk communication was perceived as a one-way process, in which experts informed the public about hazards. In contrast, contemporary risk communication prioritises collaboration, engagement, and two-way dialogue, acknowledging that risk perceptions are influenced by psychological, social, and cultural factors (Balog-Way et al., 2020).

One of the primary goals of risk communication is to ensure that public perceptions are consistent with evidence-based risk assessments (Rakow et al., 2015; Lundgren & McMakin, 2013). The public's perception of hazards frequently differs from the actual probabilities, which is one of the most significant obstacles to security risk management. Security professionals can assist the public in comprehending the distinction between genuine and exaggerated risks by furnishing them with precise, comprehensible, and pertinent risk information.

An additional critical objective is to promote appropriate risk mitigation behaviours at both the individual and organisational levels (Frewer, 2004). The mere presentation of risk facts is insufficient; practical guidance and motivation are required to encourage individuals and businesses to implement protective measures. For instance, numerous individuals acknowledge that cybersecurity risks are posed by insecure passwords and phishing assaults; however, they neglect to implement best practices, such as two-factor authentication. Therefore, risk communication must be developed to not only inform but also inspire action by means of persuasive messaging, behavioural prompting, and explicit risk mitigation guidelines.

Successful risk communication necessitates trust and credibility (Brecher & Flynn, 2002; Renn & Levine, 1991). The perceived veracity of the source conveying the message significantly influences public compliance with security measures. People are more inclined to adhere to risk mitigation recommendations from sources that they regard as transparent, knowledgeable, and consistent with their values. Institutions that maintain consistent, transparent, and empathetic communication foster a greater sense of public confidence, which in turn improves security preparedness and crisis response. As a result, risk communication is not solely about the dissemination of expert knowledge; it is also about the cultivation of an environment in which scientific discoveries, societal values, and individual motivations can coexist in a shared comprehension of how to address evolving threats.

Risk communication is a critical component of security management, as it affects the comprehension, evaluation, and mitigation of risks by both individuals and organisations. Insight into the processing of risk messages and the responses of various audiences to security concerns is provided by a variety of theoretical frameworks. These models provide insights into the cognitive, social, and cultural aspects of risk communication.

One of the earliest frameworks for risk communication is the Information Deficit Model. It is predicated on the premise that risk misperceptions are the result of a dearth of knowledge and that the provision of factual information will result in improved decision-making and behavioural adjustments (Ko, 2016).

This paradigm presupposes a linear transmission of information from specialists to the public, whereby the acquisition of more knowledge results in the ability to make informed and rational decisions. The model's limited applicability in real-world contexts is underscored by subsequent critiques, which emphasise that the public rarely interprets expert data in a vacuum. An excessive reliance on the deficit viewpoint can result in communicators placing blame on the audience for "ignorance" rather than recognising the intricate interplay of historical factors, social context, and trust that shapes public attitudes (Kasperson et al., 1988). Consequently, while it is imperative to provide data that is both explicit and accessible, this alone does not ensure that expert and casual risk perceptions are in alignment.

The Mental Models Approach emphasises that individuals possess pre-existing beliefs, values, and conceptual frameworks regarding risks, thereby resolving numerous deficiencies in the Information Deficit Model. Advocates of this perspective contend that effective communication necessitates comprehension of these vernacular mental models in order to identify discrepancies between expert assessments and public interpretations (Gibson et al., 2016; Holtrop et al., 2021). The mapping of these mental models entails the use of qualitative and quantitative methods, such as surveys, focus groups, and interviews, to clarify how individuals conceptualise the sources, pathways, and consequences of potential hazards. With these insights at their disposal, communicators can develop interventions that are specifically designed to resolve misconceptions or knowledge gaps.

Risk perception is not exclusively a cognitive process; it is also influenced by cultural and social factors. According to the Cultural Cognition Framework, risk perception is a profoundly social process, as individuals interpret risks based on their ideological and group affiliations (Renn & Benighaus, 2013). Advocates of this framework contend that individuals' beliefs regarding risk are frequently correlated with their broader ideological or cultural orientations (Kahan et al., 2012). This realisation has practical implications for the customisation of messages: communicators must recognise that uniform messaging may be unsuccessful if it is in conflict with the cultural obligations of specific demographic segments.

In all of these theoretical models, trust and credibility are consistently identified as critical determinants of effective risk communication. Research has demonstrated that audiences are more inclined to embrace recommendations when they regard communicators—whether they are government agencies, scientific experts, or media outlets—as trustworthy (Mihelj et al., 2022). The communicator's reputation and perceived expertise are crucial, but trust-building should also include transparent disclosure of potential conflicts of interest, limitations, and methodologies, in addition to credentials.

The interpretation, evaluation, and response to security concerns of individuals are influenced by the framing of risk messages, which is a fundamental strategy in risk communication. The efficacy of risk communication is contingent upon the content of the message and the manner in which it is presented, as various framing strategies can elicit distinct cognitive and emotive responses.

Loss-framed messages emphasise the negative repercussions of inaction, such as "Failing to secure your account makes you vulnerable to cybercriminals," while gain-framed messages emphasise the positive outcomes of taking preventive actions, such as "Using strong passwords protects your sensitive data" (O'Keefe & Jensen, 2008; O'Keefe & Jensen, 2009).

Prospect theory posits that individuals are risk-averse when outcomes are framed positively and risk-seeking when confronted with potential losses, which is the psychological mechanism that underpins framing effects (Kahneman & Tversky, 1979). While a loss frame may be more captivating, it may also evoke defensiveness, particularly if the recipients feel impotent to avert negative repercussions. In order to accomplish both a sense of agency among the audience and clarity of potential hazards, effective risk communication necessitates the careful balance of these frames.

Another fundamental principle of framing is the establishment of an appropriate equilibrium between rational arguments and emotive appeals (Loewenstein et al., 2001). Emotional language, such as fear-based appeals, can mobilise rapid action by emphasising the severity of a threat. Nevertheless, if individuals perceive the situation as uncontrollable, an excessive reliance on fear may result in anxiety or disengagement. As a result, the integration of evidence-based information and emotional resonance is effective in conveying urgency and providing recipients with practical solutions. This dual approach guarantees that recipients are both motivated to alter their behaviour and acknowledge the feasibility of doing so.

Risk messages are not equally effective for all audiences. The perception and response of individuals to security hazards are significantly influenced by demographic, cultural, and situational factors. According to research, the evaluation of risk messages by individuals is influenced by their age, education level, prior experience, and personal values (Cheng et al., 2011). Consequently, the varied backgrounds, priorities, and experiences of various audience segments must also be taken into account in order to effectively frame risk messages (Johnston et al., 2018). In culturally diverse environments, it is necessary to consider potential differences in communication styles, values, and norms when employing language, metaphors, and visuals.

Although risk message framing is a potent instrument, it also raises ethical concerns, particularly in the context of sensationalism, fear-based messaging, and misinformation. The utilisation of highly emotional appeals, such as exaggerated security threats or apocalyptic language, has the potential to erode public trust in security authorities and increase public apprehension (Walsh, 2020).

Misinformation and the dissemination of deceptive security narratives should also be addressed in practical risk communication strategies. In the digital era, the amplification of misinformation has been accelerated by social media, which has made it more difficult to convey precise risk messages. Organisations must employ trusted couriers, such as scientific institutions and security experts, to actively combat misinformation by providing fact-based corrections and credible sources (Kasperson & Kasperson, 2012).

An additional critical factor is the potential for risk communication to perpetuate social inequalities. Language barriers, digital divides, or lower levels of formal education may result in a lack of access to risk information for specific populations, such as lower-income communities or non-native speakers, according to research (Guttman, 2017). Consequently, effective ethical risk communication must be inclusive, guaranteeing that all members of society have equal access to security information. This can be accomplished by employing plain language, providing translations, and engaging with a variety of media platforms to reach marginalised groups (Cheng et al., 2011).

Media and technology are instrumental in determining the manner in which risks are communicated and comprehended. Information regarding potential hazards can be either emphasised or mitigated through a variety of mediums, including newspaper articles, televised broadcasts, and social media trends. This underscores the necessity of strategic, evidence-based engagement by risk communicators and security practitioners, as these processes have profound implications for public awareness, trust, and policy response (Kasperson et al., 1988).

Historically, newspapers, television, and radio were the primary gatekeepers of information. Agenda-setting is a phenomenon that is commonly observed in newspapers and broadcast journalism, where the selection of stories to feature and the prominence of those stories are determined. This dynamic has tangible consequences for public perception and policy priorities, as certain hazards are given greater prominence while others are disregarded (McCombs et al., 2014). The risk landscape can be distorted by the overemphasis of extraordinary or extreme events, which can lead communities to prioritise low-probability hazards over more statistically significant threats (Vasterman, 2018). The delicate equilibrium that legacy media entities must maintain when covering security and risk issues is underscored by the tension between the desire for compelling stories and the need for informative reporting.

The manner in which risk messages are communicated and received has been significantly altered by the proliferation of digital platforms and social media. Social media platforms, including Twitter, Facebook, and YouTube, enable individuals to engage in discussions, challenge official narratives, and seek clarification, in contrast to traditional media, which operates on a one-way information dissemination model (Tsoy et al., 2021). Social media is especially advantageous for real-time risk communication during emergencies, including security vulnerabilities or public safety concerns, due to its interactive nature. Furthermore, social media analytics enable communicators to monitor public sentiment and responses to risk messages, thereby enabling them to optimise their strategies in accordance with audience engagement.

Nevertheless, social media also poses substantial risks, particularly in the context of misinformation and echo chambers. The rapid dissemination of unverified claims, conspiracy theories, and fraudulent security alerts has the potential to erode public confidence in legitimate warnings

(Shahbazi & Bunker, 2024). In online echo chambers, where like-minded communities reinforce unverified narratives, fabricated claims can propagate widely (Del Vicario et al., 2016; Törnberg, 2018). As a result, the viral propagation of conspiracy theories or rumours can undermine the credibility of legitimate expertise and disrupt coherent response strategies.

It is imperative to incorporate a variety of media strategies in order to ensure effective risk communication, as both traditional and digital media have their own strengths and limitations. A multi-channel approach guarantees that risk messages are conveyed to a wide range of audiences via various platforms, thereby enhancing the retention and comprehension of the message.

Conclusion

In security management, effective risk communication is essential to ensure that individuals and organisations comprehend, evaluate, and respond appropriately to threats. This chapter emphasises the impact of psychological, social, and cultural factors on the perception and response to risk. Communicators can customise messages that resonate with a wide range of audiences, thereby addressing misconceptions and fostering evidence-based comprehension, by utilising theoretical models such as the Information Deficit Model, the Mental Models Approach, and the Cultural Cognition Framework.

Trust and credibility continue to be indispensable components of effective risk communication. In order to preserve public trust in security measures, it is imperative to adopt ethical considerations, expertise, and transparency. In order to prevent fear-based disengagement, it is imperative that risk messages be articulated with precision to strike a balance between urgency and empowerment. Furthermore, inclusive and equitable communication strategies are guaranteed by acknowledging demographic and cultural distinctions.

Media and technology are becoming more influential in the development of risk narratives. Although social media enables the rapid dissemination of information and engagement, it also presents obstacles in the form of misinformation and echo chambers. In order to improve public awareness and security preparedness, a multi-channel strategy is necessary for effective risk communication, which combines traditional and digital platforms.

Ultimately, the development of a proactive risk communication culture, which is based on trust, adaptability, and inclusivity, fortifies security resilience and guarantees that risk management initiatives are both ethically sound and effective.

REFERENCES

Balog-Way, D., McComas, K., & Besley, J. (2020). The evolving field of risk communication. *Risk Analysis, 40*(S1).

Brecher, R., & Flynn, T. (2002). *Principles of risk communicationbuilding trust and credibility with the public* (pp. 447–457). Elsevier eBooks.

Cheng, T., Woon, D. K., & Lynes, J. K. (2011). The use of message framing in the promotion of environmentally sustainable behaviors. *Social Marketing Quarterly, 17*(2), 48–62.

Del Vicario, M., Bessi, A., Zollo, F., Petroni, F., Scala, A., Caldarelli, G., Stanley, H. E., & Quattrociocchi, W. (2016). The spreading of misinformation online. *Proceedings of the National Academy of Sciences, 113*(3), 554–559.

Fischhoff, B. (1995). Risk perception and communication unplugged: Twenty years of process. *Risk Analysis, 15*(2), 137–145.

Frewer, L. (2004). The public and effective risk communication. *Toxicology Letters, 149*(1–3), 391–397.

Gibson, H., Stewart, I. S., Pahl, S., & Stokes, A. (2016). A 'mental models' approach to the communication of subsurface hydrology and hazards. *Hydrology and Earth System Sciences, 20*(5), 1737–1749.

Guttman, N. (2017). *Ethical issues in health promotion and communication interventions*. Oxford Research Encyclopedia of Communication.

Holtrop, J. S., Scherer, L. D., Matlock, D. D., Glasgow, R. E., & Green, L. A. (2021). The importance of mental models in implementation science. *Frontiers in Public Health, 9*(1).

Johnston, A. C., Warkentin, M., Dennis, A. R., & Siponen, M. (2018). Speak their language: Designing effective messages to improve employees' information security decision making. *Decision Sciences, 50*(2), 245–284.

Kahan, D. M., Peters, E., Wittlin, M., Slovic, P., Ouellette, L. L., Braman, D., & Mandel, G. (2012). The polarizing impact of science literacy and numeracy on perceived climate change risks. *Nature Climate Change, 2*(10), 732–735.

Kahneman, D., & Tversky, A. (1979). Prospect theory: An analysis of decision under risk. *Econometrica, 47*(2), 263–292.

Kasperson, R. E., & Kasperson, J. (2012). *Social contours of risk*. Routledge.

Kasperson, R. E., Renn, O., Slovic, P., Brown, H. S., Emel, J., Goble, R., Kasperson, J. X., & Ratick, S. (1988). The social amplification of risk: A conceptual framework. *Risk Analysis, 8*(2), 177–187.

Ko, H. (2016). In science communication, why does the idea of a public deficit always return? How do the shifting information flows in healthcare affect the deficit model of science communication? *Public Understanding of Science, 25*(4), 427–432.

Loewenstein, G. F., Weber, E. U., Hsee, C. K., & Welch, N. (2001). Risk as feelings. *Psychological Bulletin, 127*(2), 267–286.

Lundgren, R. E., & McMakin, A. H. (2013). *Risk communication*. John Wiley & Sons Inc.

McCombs, M. E., Shaw, D. L., & Weaver, D. H. (2014). New directions in agenda-setting theory and research. *Mass Communication and Society, 17*(6), 781–802.

Mihelj, S., Kondor, K., & Štětka, V. (2022). Establishing trust in experts during a crisis: Expert trustworthiness and media use during the COVID-19 pandemic. *Science Communication, 44*(3), 107554702211005.

O'Keefe, D. J., & Jensen, J. D. (2008). Do loss-framed persuasive messages engender greater message processing than do gain-framed messages? A meta-analytic review. *Communication Studies, 59*(1), 51–67.

O'Keefe, D. J., & Jensen, J. D. (2009). The relative persuasiveness of gain-framed and loss-framed messages for encouraging disease detection behaviors: A meta-analytic review. *Journal of Communication, 59*(2), 296–316.

Rakow, T., Heard, C. L., & Newell, B. R. (2015). Meeting three challenges in risk communication: Phenomena, numbers, and emotions. *Policy Insights from the Behavioral and Brain Sciences, 2*(1), 147–156.

Renn, O., & Benighaus, C. (2013). Perception of technological risk: Insights from research and lessons for risk communication and management. *Journal of Risk Research, 16*(3–4), 293–313.

Renn, O., & Levine, D. (1991). Credibility and trust in risk communication. *Communicating Risks to the Public, 4*, 175–217.

Shahbazi, M., & Bunker, D. (2024). Social media trust: Fighting misinformation in the time of crisis. *International Journal of Information Management, 77*(102780), 102780–102780.

Slovic, P. (Ed.). (2000). *The perception of risk*. Earthscan Publications.

Törnberg, P. (2018) Echo chambers and viral misinformation: Modeling fake news as complex contagion. *PLOS ONE, 13*(9).

Tsoy, D., Tirasawasdichai, T., & Kurpayanidi, K. I. (2021). Role of social media in shaping public risk perception during COVID-19 pandemic: A theoretical review. *International Journal of Management Science and Business Administration, 7*(2), 35–41.

Vasterman, P. (2018). *From media hype to Twitter storm*. Amsterdam University Press.

Walsh, J. P. (2020). Social media and moral panics: Assessing the effects of technological change on societal reaction. *International Journal of Cultural Studies, 23*(6), 840–859.

PART II

Psychology

CHAPTER 5

Psychological Theories in the Context of Security

Abstract This chapter delves into the role of psychological theories in security, with a particular emphasis on the cognitive, social, and emotional factors that influence security behaviour. Cognitive psychology emphasises the impact of cognitive burden, fallacies, and heuristics on risk perception and decision-making. Social psychology investigates the influence of group dynamics, conformity, and diffusion of responsibility on security culture. Compliance with security protocols is influenced by emotional and motivational factors, such as tension and fear-based messaging. Organisations can develop effective security strategies that promote proactive security behaviour, enhance resilience, and mitigate risks by incorporating these psychological perspectives. It is imperative to comprehend these factors in order to enhance security frameworks and mitigate human-related risks in physical and digital security environments.

Keywords Cognitive load · Attention and memory constraints · Group dynamics · Motivation and emotions · Heuristic errors

Introduction

Psychological theories offer valuable insights into the cognitive biases, decision-making, and human behaviour that influence security practices. It is imperative to comprehend the manner in which individuals interact with social environments, respond to threats, and process information in order to create effective security measures.

Cognitive psychology investigates the manner in which individuals assess and perceive risks, frequently employing heuristics—mental shortcuts that can result in security vulnerabilities. Cognitive fatigue, anchoring bias, and optimism bias all contribute to poor decision-making, which in turn increases the likelihood of falling victim to phishing schemes and social engineering attacks. Security professionals must consider these cognitive limitations when developing risk assessments and awareness programmes. Social psychology investigates the ways in which security behaviour is influenced by group dynamics and authority. The security culture of an organisation can be weakened by conformity, groupthink, and the diffusion of responsibility, thereby increasing its susceptibility to threats. These hazards can be mitigated by promoting accountability and critical thinking within teams. Security behaviour is additionally influenced by motivation and emotions. Cognitive performance is impaired by stress and exhaustion, which results in lapses in vigilance and adherence to security protocols. In order to encourage compliance, it is imperative to carefully balance empowerment strategies with fear-based security messaging. Organisations can enhance security policies, mitigate vulnerabilities, and foster a proactive security culture by incorporating cognitive, social, and emotive psychological perspectives.

Cognitive psychology is the empirical examination of the manner in which individuals think, learn, and comprehend information (Eysenck and Keane, 2020). It investigates the processes by which individuals acquire and apply knowledge, as well as the manner in which they make decisions. Cognitive psychology can assist in the description of human behaviour and the enhancement of memory and learning abilities. It offers invaluable insights into the manner in which individuals process information, particularly in the presence of tension and uncertainty. It is essential to comprehend these processes in the context of security, as cognitive limitations frequently exacerbate vulnerabilities to threats, including deception and other types of intrusions.

The mental effort necessary to comprehend information and complete duties is referred to as cognitive load. In high-stress security environments, the cognitive burden can become overwhelming, resulting in increased error rates and impaired judgement (Endsley, 1995). Research has demonstrated that individuals who are under a high cognitive load are more susceptible to deceptive emails, as they are unable to comprehensively evaluate the content due to a dearth of mental resources (Vishwanath et al., 2011). For example, in work environments where employees are required to process large volumes of email, the probability of identifying subtle inconsistencies in phishing messages, such as misspelt URLs or suspicious attachments, is diminished by fatigue and time constraints. Cognitive resources are subject to a constant demand for vigilance in identifying anomalies in data or communications, which results in diminished performance and an increased susceptibility to threats. The mere volume of data and the urgency of the situation can impede decision-making, rendering cognitive overload particularly hazardous in scenarios that necessitate a rapid response.

Attention and memory are fundamental cognitive processes that have a substantial impact on security-related behaviour. Memory enables the retention and retrieval of information, while attention enables individuals to concentrate on particular stimuli. In environments with incessant distractions, critical signals are frequently disregarded due to limited attentional capacity. For example, fraudulent emails frequently capitalise on attentional lapses by incorporating malicious links into visually dense or time-sensitive messages. Williams et al. (2018) have conducted research that indicates that users are considerably more susceptible to phishing attempts when they are multitasking or under time constraints. In addition, vulnerabilities are further exacerbated by memory constraints. For instance, the capacity of short-term memory to retain a finite number of items (Miller, 1956) presents a challenge for individuals who wish to recall intricate security protocols or recognise hazards that they have previously encountered.

Cognition is distinguished by its capacity to anticipate. Decision-making is significantly influenced by inferences regarding future events, which allow us to anticipate and optimise our actions in order to mitigate damage and reap rewards. Given the significance of these future projections, it is reasonable to anticipate that the brain would possess precise, impartial foresight. Nevertheless, decision-making frequently transpires in the presence of time constraints and uncertainty, which induces individuals to depend on cognitive shortcuts referred to as heuristics. Although heuristics may be effective, they frequently result in systematic errors in risk perception. Humans demonstrate a pervasive and unexpected bias: when it comes to predicting the future, we overestimate the likelihood of positive events and underestimate the likelihood of negative events (Sharot, 2011). This phenomenon is referred to as the optimism bias, and it is one of the most robust, consistent, and prevalent biases that have been documented in the fields of psychology and behavioural economics.

Furthermore, the availability heuristic causes individuals to overestimate the probability of events that are readily recollected (Tversky & Kahneman, 1974), such as widely publicised cyberattacks, while underestimating less salient but equally probable hazards. Similarly, the anchoring bias, which Furnham and Boo (2011) define as "a process by which individuals are influenced by specific information provided prior to a judgement," has the potential to distort risk assessments. For instance, if an initial threat assessment understates the risk, subsequent evaluations may continue to be biassed towards the original figure, despite the presence of new evidence.

Research indicates that security vulnerabilities are frequently not solely technical failures, but rather are exacerbated by flawed human decision-making within organisational and social structures (Lipatov, 2014). Social psychology investigates the ways in which social interactions and group membership affect the thoughts, emotions, and behaviours of individuals. Social psychology is fundamentally concerned with the manner in which individuals think, experience, and behave in the presence of others (Fiske et al., 2010). The behaviour of individuals within organisations, teams, and broader social structures is directly influenced by critical components of social psychology, such as group dynamics, authority, and identity, which in turn affect security outcomes. These psychological processes have the potential to either enhance security practices by encouraging cooperation and adherence to rules, or introduce vulnerabilities, such as susceptibility to social engineering, groupthink, and the diffusion of responsibility. It is imperative to comprehend these social psychological influences in order to develop security frameworks that foster critical thinking, individual responsibility, and organisational resilience in the face of both deliberate security threats and human error.

Janis (1972) defines groupthink as a psychological phenomenon in which individuals prioritise group cohesion and consensus over critical evaluation, frequently resulting in flawed decision-making. Conformity, a closely related phenomenon, is the process by which individuals modify their behaviours to conform to the norms of the group. Crutchfield (1955) also defines conformity as "submitting to group pressures." It is also referred to as predominant influence. Depending on the prevailing organisational attitudes towards security practices, conformity can either bolster or erode security culture in security contexts. This is especially pertinent in security teams, where conformance pressure can suppress dissenting opinions, resulting in oversights in risk assessment or a failure to address security threats. Research suggests that individuals are less inclined to express concerns that challenge dominant narratives within a group when they are under pressure to conform (Nemeth & Goncalo, 2011).

In cybersecurity operations, where early threat detection necessitates the willingness to challenge assumptions and consider a variety of perspectives, this effect can be particularly perilous.

In order to reduce the risks associated with groupthink and conformity, organisations should implement strategies that promote structured critical thinking, open discussion, and diverse perspectives. Additionally, they should diversify their security teams to reduce homogeneity in risk assessment and perspectives. The tendency for conformity-based decision-making can be mitigated by establishing formal devil's advocate roles in security teams and cultivating a culture that values interrogating.

Diffusion of responsibility is the process by which individuals in a group presume that someone else will take action, resulting in inaction in critical situations. This phenomenon, which is frequently linked to the bystander effect, has been extensively investigated in emergency response scenarios. However, it is equally applicable to security environments. The bystander effect refers to the inclination of individuals to be less inclined to take action when others are present, presuming that one of them will intervene (Darley & Latané, 1968). This dynamic is also relevant to the reporting of security threats. For example, when multiple employees receive an alert regarding a potential phishing attack, each individual may presume that the issue has already been escalated by another individual or will notify the incident response team. The bystander effect can significantly impede threat detection in modern workplaces, despite the fact that they frequently rely on collective responsibility for security. This is due to the absence of defined accountability structures and immediate reporting mechanisms.

Organisations should implement the following measures to mitigate the bystander effect in security teams:

Ensure that reporting roles and responsibilities are clearly defined by implementing explicit security policies.
Incorporate mandatory security training to underscore the importance of personal accountability.
Employ psychological nudges, such as pop-up reminders that encourage employees to report suspicious activities.
Foster a culture of shared responsibility by incentivising proactive security engagement.

Human behaviour, such as compliance with security protocols and risk-related decision-making, is significantly influenced by emotions and motivation. Burnout and inadequate decision-making are frequently associated with high-stress environments, which, in turn, exacerbate security vulnerabilities (Nobles, 2022). Stress and exhaustion have a substantial impact on cognitive performance, decision-making, and adherence to standard security protocols. Stress is a condition in which an individual perceives the demands of an environmental stimulus as exceeding their capacity to meet, mitigate, or modify those demands, as per Lazarus et al. (1985). Chronic stress, particularly in high-stakes security environments, can result in an increased likelihood of errors, impaired risk assessment, and reduced vigilance (McEwen, 2007).

Cognitive fatigue is a common occurrence among security professionals, including cyber analysts, emergency responders, and corporate security personnel, who frequently operate under high pressure. According to research, protracted tension can have a detrimental impact on working memory, problem-solving abilities, and situational awareness, which can ultimately compromise security defences (Arnsten, 2009). Burnout, a condition that is defined by emotional exhaustion, depersonalisation, and diminished personal accomplishment, can result from chronic stress (Maslach et al., 2001). Cognitive resources are depleted when individuals are persistently stressed or worn out. Consequently, they may encounter difficulty in maintaining the sustained attention necessary to verify alerts or monitor systems. Critical indicators of social engineering attempts or insider threats may be overlooked as a result of such lapses.

Mitigation strategies involve the integration of stress reduction techniques, such as mindfulness, relaxation exercises, and burden balancing, into security training. Additionally, mental health support programmes that are specifically designed for security personnel are encouraged. In addition, research indicates that burnout rates among high-stress professionals are significantly reduced by workload management, flexible scheduling, and appropriate personnel (Demerouti et al., 2001). These measures not only improve well-being but also strengthen the collective ability to effectively identify and respond to security concerns.

Fear is one of the most potent emotional motivators in the context of security decision-making. For example, the temporary increase in security awareness and adherence to policies may be facilitated by fear appeals, such as warnings regarding the severe repercussions of data breaches. In controlled quantities, dread can serve as an incentive for users to verify suspicious emails or update their passwords more frequently. Fear can be a motivator for adhering to security protocols; however, excessive fear can result in irrational decision-making, overreaction to threats, or even avoidance behaviours (Loewenstein et al., 2001).

In contrast, security awareness campaigns that are based on dread may be effective in the short term, but they may diminish in effectiveness over time or even backfire. According to Witte's Extended Parallel Process Model (EPPM), individuals are more inclined to disengage rather than implement proactive measures when they perceive a security threat as overwhelming and beyond their control (Witte, 1992). In order to reduce adverse consequences, it is necessary to balance fear appeals with efficacy messaging, which provides users with information on how to effectively safeguard themselves (Witte & Allen, 2000). Organisations enable individuals to transform their anxiety or denial into constructive security behaviours by combining warnings with actionable actions (e.g., "Report suspicious links," "Use two-factor authentication").

Security behaviour is significantly influenced by motivation. Employees do not adhere to security policies solely because they are instructed to do so; rather, they comply when security measures are in accordance with their personal and organisational objectives. Organisations can develop effective policies and incentives by comprehending the reasons why individuals adhere to or disregard security protocols. Security adherence may be motivated by intrinsic factors (such as personal interest or ethical commitment) or extrinsic factors (such as rewards, recognition, or fear of penalties). Intrinsic motivation is generally more sustainable, as individuals who perceive security practices as meaningful are more likely to maintain consistent vigilance (Ryan & Deci, 2000). In contrast, compliance may be achieved solely when incentives are present, as opposed to relying exclusively on extrinsic motivation (e.g., monetary rewards) (Frey & Jegen, 2001).

Self-Determination Theory (SDT) argues that humans possess fundamental requirements for autonomy, competence, and relatedness (Ryan & Deci, 2000). In security contexts, employees' engagement and ownership of security practices are enhanced by the provision of some autonomy, such as the ability to select their preferable training modules. The development of a sense of self-efficacy is facilitated by the provision of opportunities for competence-building, such as advanced security seminars, while the cultivation of a collaborative organisational culture enhances relatedness. Secure behaviours can be reinforced through the implementation of reward systems that are meticulously crafted. Positive reinforcement can be achieved by publicly acknowledging employees who promptly report anomalies or detect phishing attempts.

Conclusion

This chapter emphasises the importance of psychological theories in comprehending security-related behaviours. Cognitive psychology emphasises the role of memory, attention, and information processing limitations in the development of vulnerabilities, including susceptibility to phishing and decision-making blunders under high cognitive burden. Heuristic fallacies, such as optimism bias and anchoring bias, further corrupt risk perception, resulting in flawed security judgements.

Social psychology offers a perspective on the ways in which security culture is influenced by group dynamics, conformity, and the diffusion of responsibility. Strategies that promote critical thinking and accountability are necessary due to the potential for groupthink and the bystander effect to undermine proactive security measures. In order to mitigate these psychological hazards, organisational structures must prioritise structured decision-making, explicit reporting responsibilities, and a variety of perspectives.

Additionally, security adherence is significantly influenced by motivation and emotions. Cognitive performance is impaired by stress and exhaustion, which increases the probability of security breaches. In order to prevent disengagement, it is imperative to balance fear-based security messaging with actionable solutions. According to motivational theories, the promotion of intrinsic motivation, autonomy, and competence can improve adherence to security policies.

The integration of cognitive, social, and emotive psychological insights can be used to design security frameworks that promote proactive security behaviours, enhance resilience, and reduce vulnerabilities. It is imperative to adopt a comprehensive approach to psychological factors in order to create sustainable and effective security strategies.

References

Arnsten, A. (2009). Stress signalling pathways that impair prefrontal cortex structure and function. *Nature Reviews Neuroscience, 10*, 410–422.

Crutchfield, R. S. (1955). Conformity and character. *American Psychologist, 10*(5), 191–198.

Darley, J. M., & Latane, B. (1968). Bystander intervention in emergencies: Diffusion of responsibility. *Journal of Personality and Social Psychology, 8*(4, Pt.1), 377–383.

Demerouti, E., Bakker, A. B., Nachreiner, F., & Schaufeli, W. B. (2001). The job demands-resources model of burnout. *Journal of Applied Psychology, 86*(3), 499–512.

Endsley, M. R. (1995). Toward a theory of situation awareness in dynamic systems. *Human Factors, 37*(1), 32–64.

Eysenck, M. W., & Keane, M. T. (2020) *Cognitive psychology: A student's handbook*. Psychology press.

Fiske, S. T., Gilbert, D. T., & Lindzey, G. (Eds.). (2010). *Handbook of social psychology* (5th ed.). Wiley.

Furnham, A., & Boo, H. C. (2011). A literature review of the anchoring effect. *The Journal of Socio-Economics, 40*(1), 35–42.

Frey, B. S., & Jegen, R. (2001). Motivation crowding theory. *Journal of Economic Surveys, 15*(5), 589–611.

Janis, I. L. (1972). *Victims of groupthink: A psychological study of foreign-policy decisions and fiascoes*. Houghton Mifflin.

Lazarus, R. S., DeLongis, A., Folkman, S., & Gruen, R. (1985). Stress and adaptational outcomes. The problem of confounded measures. *American Psychologist, 40*(7), 770–785.

Lipatov, V. (2014). *Compliance dynamics generated by social interaction rules (No. 4767)* (CESifo Working Paper).

Loewenstein, G. F., Weber, E. U., Hsee, C. K., & Welch, N. (2001). Risk as feelings. *Psychological Bulletin, 127*(2), 267–286.

Maslach, C., Schaufeli, W. B., & Leiter, M. P. (2001). Job burnout. *Annual Review of Psychology, 52*, 397–422.

McEwen, B. S. (2007). Physiology and neurobiology of stress and adaptation: Central role of the brain. *Physiological Reviews, 87*(3), 873–904.

Miller, G. A. (1956). The magical number seven, plus or minus two: Some limits on our capacity for processing information. *Psychological Review, 63*(2), 81–97.

Nemeth, C. J., & Goncalo, J. A. (2011). Rogues and heroes: Finding value in dissent. *Current Directions in Psychological Science, 20*(1), 46–50.

Nobles, C. (2022). Stress, burnout, and security fatigue in cybersecurity: A human factors problem. *Holistica–Journal of Business and Public Administration, 13*, 49–72.

Ryan, R. M., & Deci, E. L. (2000). Self-determination theory and the facilitation of intrinsic motivation, social development, and well-being. *American Psychologist, 55*(1), 68–78.

Sharot, T. (2011). The optimism bias. *Current Biology, 21*(23), R941–R945.

Tversky, A., & Kahneman, D. (1974) Judgment under uncertainty: Heuristics and biases. *Science, 185*(4157), 1124–1131.

Vishwanath, A., Herath, T., Chen, R., Wang, J., & Rao, H. R. (2011). Why do people get phished? Testing individual differences in phishing vulnerability within an integrated. *Information Processing Model. Decision Support Systems, 51*(3), 576–586.

Williams, M., Hinds, J., & Joinson, A. (2018). Exploring susceptibility to phishing in the workplace. *Cyberpsychology, Behavior, and Social Networking, 21*(7), 441–446.

Witte, K. (1992). Putting the fear back into fear appeals: The extended parallel process model. *Communication Monographs, 59*(4), 329–349.

Witte, K., & Allen, M. (2000). A meta-analysis of fear appeals: Implications for effective public health campaigns. *Health Education & Behavior, 27*(5), 591–615.

CHAPTER 6

Profiling and the Psychological Characteristics of Criminals

Abstract This chapter investigates the psychological characteristics and motivations that underlie security-related crimes, including insider threats and cybercrime. In relation to criminal behaviour, the Dark Triad (narcissism, psychopathy, and Machiavellianism) are examined as critical personality constructs. Offender actions are additionally influenced by motivational motivations, including ideology, personal grievances, and financial incentives. Furthermore, the chapter addresses criminal profiling methodologies, which incorporate psychological assessments and behavioural analytics. Ethical concerns, such as potential biases and privacy violations, are critically evaluated. This chapter emphasises the necessity of ethical and evidence-based approaches while also offering insights into crime prevention and security strategies through the examination of offender psychology and profiling techniques.

Introduction

Psychological characteristics that influence ethical disregard, risk-taking, and deception are what shape criminal behaviour in security-related contexts, including cybercrime and insider threats. Law enforcement and security professionals are able to identify and mitigate threats by comprehending these characteristics.

The Dark Triad—narcissism, psychopathy, and Machiavellianism—is a critical characteristic of offenders, as indicated by research. These individuals are characterised by a lack of empathy, impulsivity, and manipulativeness, which contributes to criminal behaviour. Furthermore, offences are motivated by personal grievances, ideology, financial gain, and intellectual challenge.

Initially devised for violent offences, criminal profiling has since expanded to encompass cybercrime and insider threats. Behavioural analytics, psychological assessments, and AI-driven threat detection are all components of contemporary profiling techniques. Nevertheless, profiling raises ethical concerns, such as potential discrimination and privacy violations.

This chapter investigates the psychological characteristics and motivations that underlie security-related criminal activities, as well as profiling methodologies. It addresses the ethical implications of profiling while providing insights into offender behaviour by investigating the intersection of criminal intent and personality. It is imperative to maintain security without violating fundamental liberties through a balanced approach.

Psychological attributes that influence decision-making and risk-taking tendencies significantly influence criminal behaviour, particularly in cybercrime and insider threats. Research in forensic and cyberpsychology has identified several critical traits that are commonly associated with security-related criminals, including narcissism, psychopathy, and Machiavellianism, which are collectively known as the Dark Triad (Paulhus & Williams, 2002). Individuals are more susceptible to illicit or deviant behaviour as a result of these characteristics, which contribute to deception, exploitation, and a lack of ethical constraint.

Narcissistic individuals demonstrate a lack of empathy, a profound desire for admiration, a propensity to exploit others for self-gain, and an inflated sense of self-importance (Raskin & Terry, 1988). In cybercriminal contexts, narcissism can be characterised by a strong conviction in one's own superiority, such as the belief that offenders are more intelligent or capable than both potential victims and law enforcement. This exaggerated self-perception may result in them underestimating risks and overestimating their capacity to evade detection.

Impulsivity, superficial charisma, manipulativeness, and a lack of remorse or empathy are all characteristics of psychopathy (Hare, 1999). In contrast to narcissists, psychopaths are more pragmatic and goal-oriented in their criminal activities, frequently engaging in ransomware attacks, identity theft, and fraud with minimal consideration for the well-being of their victims. Psychopaths in security breaches exploit human vulnerabilities by employing deception and charisma to circumvent security controls (2006) (Babiak & Hare).

Machiavellians prioritise self-interest, deception, and manipulation over moral or ethical considerations (Christie & Geis, 1970). Machiavellian offenders are adept at manipulating social and technological systems, whether by executing intricate "social engineering" schemes, orchestrating insider collusion, or constructing spear-phishing campaigns (Padayachee, 2021). They are adept at utilising systems for personal or organisational advantage, frequently meticulously plotting security breaches. Machiavellian cybercriminals strategically manipulate others to perpetrate security violations, in contrast to impulsive offenders.

Security-related criminals exhibit distinctive behavioural patterns that are determined by their motivations, personality traits, and group affiliations. Understanding these behaviours is essential for the purpose of risk profiling and mitigation. A distinctive blend of intelligence, curiosity, and risk-taking behaviour is frequently demonstrated by cybercriminals, including hackers (Kranenbarg et al., 2022). Rather than for financial gain, numerous individuals participate in cyberattacks as an intellectual challenge (Fedoseeva, 2022). The psychological satisfaction they experience from circumventing security protocols frequently surpasses any apprehension regarding legal repercussions (Mitnick & Simon, 2003).

Unlike external criminals, insider threats are the result of individuals within an organisation who abuse their access privileges to take data, sabotage systems, or perpetrate fraud. Organisational dissatisfaction, personal grievances, or financial incentives frequently influence their motivations and behavioural patterns. Greitzer et al. (2013) have identified numerous behavioural indicators of insider risk, including the following: Disregard for Authority, Disgruntlement, Stress, and Disengagement.

Organised cybercrime syndicates are distinguished from individual hackers by their hierarchical structure, which frequently engages in financially motivated cyberattacks, fraud, and extortion schemes (Broadhurst et al., 2014). Albanese (2014) and Sidanius and Pratto (1999) have observed that these groups exhibit unique psychological and social characteristics that bolster their criminal activities. These characteristics include a high level of loyalty and commitment to criminal networks, as well as a social dominance orientation that reinforces power structures within criminal groups.

Motivational vacuums are uncommon in the context of security-related offences. The actions of perpetrators, whether they are sophisticated cybercriminals, disgruntled insiders, or members of organised hacking groups, are typically the result of underlying psychological, social, and ideological motivations. Although criminals' psychological characteristics offer a glimpse into their character, their motivations elucidate the reasons they act in accordance with their inclinations. The motivations of criminals are diverse, ranging from financial incentives to ideological activism, vengeance, psychological gratification, and peer influences.

Financial gain is a prevalent motivation for cybercrime and security-related offences, particularly in the context of insider threats, fraud, and hacking. Ransomware attacks, financial fraud, and phishing schemes are among the activities in which numerous cybercriminals participate with the primary objective of generating financial gain (Hutchings & Holt, 2015). Furthermore, the probability of traceability and prosecution is diminished by anonymous payment methods, such as cryptocurrency, which further facilitate financial crime (Kshetri, 2010).

Some cybercriminals are motivated by ideological or political reasons in addition to personal gain. Hacktivist organisations employ their technological capabilities to further their objectives, specifically targeting entities that they regard as antagonistic to their cause (Romagna & Leukfeldt, 2024). These actions, which are all intended to promote their ideological beliefs or draw attention to specific issues, can range from defacing websites to launching distributed denial-of-service (DDoS) attacks. Although some hacktivists regard themselves as freedom fighters, others violate ethical boundaries, thereby jeopardising national security and individual privacy (Karagiannopoulos, 2018).

Occasionally, crimes are motivated by personal grievances, workplace dissatisfaction, or interpersonal conflicts (Brooks & Barry-Walsh, 2022; Greenberg, 1990). Sabotage, data breaches, or fraud may be implemented by employees who perceive themselves as being neglected, underappreciated, or wrongfully terminated in an effort to exact revenge. In certain instances, the perpetrator justifies the act as a form of retribution or justice, thereby effectively distancing themselves from the ethical and legal ramifications of their actions (Bandura, 2016).

Some cybercriminals participate in security breaches and hacking not for financial or ideological gain, but for the intellectual challenge, status, or exhilaration of the crime. These offenders may also exhibit characteristics that are indicative of sensation-seeking, such as the pursuit of increasingly intricate targets and higher-risk assaults in order to achieve greater personal gratification (Zuckerman, 1994).

Criminals do not always operate in isolation. Numerous hacking collectives and cybercriminals operate within closely linked communities that exchange tools, techniques, and moral justifications for their actions (Holt, 2012). In hacker groups and cybercriminal syndicates, social reinforcement, peer validation, and collective identity are all significant factors in criminal behaviour. Criminals emulate behaviours that are observed in their communities, as per the Social Learning Theory (Bandura, 1977).

This group dynamic creates an environment in which unethical behaviour is accepted, and perpetrators may experience a diminished sense of personal accountability for collective illicit activities (Granovetter, 1978).

For years, criminal profiling has been a fundamental component of forensic psychology, assisting law enforcement in the identification, prediction, and mitigation of criminal behaviour. In security contexts, profiling techniques have advanced beyond conventional criminology by incorporating artificial intelligence (AI), psychological assessments, and behavioural analytics to identify internal threats, cybercriminal activity, and security intrusions. Nevertheless, profiling continues to be an ethically complex process that necessitates a meticulous equilibrium between security efficacy, privacy rights, and discrimination risks.

The process of criminal profiling involves the inference of offender characteristics, motives, and behavioural patterns from the nature of a crime and any available evidence (Douglas et al., 1986). Profiling, which was initially developed for violent crimes, was designed to establish a correlation between specific personal characteristics (e.g., age, emotional stability, risk tolerance) and the patterns observed at crime scenes. It has expanded to incorporate a diverse range of offences, such as terrorism, property crime, and cybercrime, over time (Chiesa et al., 2008; Martineau et al., 2023; Turvey, 2011). Profiling is designed to minimise the scope of an investigation by emphasising individuals whose behaviours or predispositions correspond to a recognised method of operation. Criminal profiling can assist in the identification of potential hazards prior to a compromise in security environments, including corporate IT departments, intelligence agencies, and financial institutions (Greitzer et al., 2012; Gill, 2015).

In security contexts, there are two primary varieties of profiling: psychological profiling and behavioural profiling. These methodologies assist organisations in the identification of prospective hazards prior to their development into comprehensive security breaches. The primary objective of behavioural profiling is to identify potential security hazards by analysing observable actions and patterns. Behavioural profiling is a security practice that entails the surveillance of user activities, including data utilisation, access patterns, and login times, in order to identify anomalies that may suggest malicious intent (Gheyas & Abdallah, 2016). Psychological profiling is a method that evaluates the likelihood of individuals perpetrating security violations by examining their mental and emotional characteristics (Turvey, 2011). Organisations can identify employees who may be at risk of engaging in malevolent activities by assessing their stress levels, motivations, and personality traits. Security applications may involve stress level assessments in high-pressure jobs, screening questionnaires for high-trust positions, or regular employee surveys.

Although psychological profiling can provide valuable insights into internal motivations (e.g., thrill-seeking or disgruntlement), it also necessitates meticulous implementation to prevent discrimination and guarantee reliability (Snook et al., 2008). In security contexts, one of the most urgent debates regarding criminal profiling is the tension between the protection of assets and the respect of individual rights (Solove, 2011).

For example, continuous behavioural monitoring may identify early indicators of insider threat activity; however, employees or users may perceive such surveillance as intrusive. Profiling inherently entails the acquisition and analysis of personal data, which can violate the privacy rights of individuals. In order to preserve trust and legitimacy, organisations must guarantee that their profiling procedures adhere to legal frameworks, including data protection laws, and adhere to ethical standards. False positives may compromise privacy or undermine morale, and not all employees who exhibit risk factors will commit an offence. Finally, profiling practices may inadvertently perpetuate biases, resulting in discrimination against specific groups (Naudts, 2019). In order to reduce these risks, organisations should establish profiling systems that are transparent, routinely audited for biases, and engineered to reduce errors.

Conclusion

This chapter emphasises the importance of comprehending the psychological characteristics of perpetrators and the fundamental motivations that drive their behaviour in order to develop an effective security strategy. This chapter emphasises the manner in which the "Dark Triad" predisposes specific individuals to deception, manipulation, and trust violations by analysing critical personality constructs, including narcissism, psychopathy, and Machiavellianism. Despite the fact that these characteristics guide criminal behaviour, the motivations of offenders—ranging from financial gain to ideological commitment or pure intellectual curiosity—are ultimately the driving force behind their decision to exploit security vulnerabilities. It is therefore essential to acknowledge the diverse personality patterns and motives that are at play in order to develop targeted mitigation strategies, such as organisational culture interventions, specialised training, and insider threat detection.

Although criminal profiling has the potential to be a powerful tool for preemptively identifying high-risk individuals or suspect behavioural patterns, it also raises complex ethical and privacy concerns. It is imperative to meticulously balance the protection of personal rights with the pursuit of security objectives when employing psychological and behavioural analytics. Behavioural monitoring and psychological evaluations are effective methods for identifying potential insider threats; however, they may result in false positives or the perpetuation of biases if not conducted with transparency and oversight. In the future, organisations should implement profiling strategies that are ethically sound, evidence-based, and informed by interdisciplinary research in psychology, criminology, and data science. This will guarantee that legitimate security requirements do not undermine fundamental human rights.

References

Albanese, J. (2014). *Organized crime*. Routledge.
Babiak, P., & Hare, R. D. (2006). *Snakes in suits: When psychopaths go to work*. Regan Books/Harper Collins Publishers.
Bandura, A. (1977). *Social learning theory*. Prentice-Hall.
Bandura, A. (2016). *Moral disengagement how people do harm and live with themselves*. New York Worth Publishers.

Broadhurst, R., Grabosky, P., Alazab, M., Bouhours, B., & Chon, S. (2014). Organizations and cybercrime. *International Journal of CyberCriminology, 8*(1), 1–20.

Brooks, N., & Barry-Walsh, J. (2022). Understanding the role of grievance and fixation in lone actor violence. *Frontiers in Psychology, 13*.

Chiesa, R., Ducci, S., & Ciappi, S. (2008). *Profiling hackers: The science of criminal profiling as applied to the world of hacking*. Taylor & Francis Ltd.

Christie, R., & Geis, F. L. (1970). *Studies in machiavellianism*. Academic Press.

Douglas, J. E., Ressler, R. K., Burgess, A. W., & Hartman, C. R. (1986). Criminal profiling from crime scene analysis. *Behavioral Sciences & the Law, 4*(4), 401–421.

Fedoseeva, O. (2022). Psychological features of the underage cybercriminal personality formation. *Legal Science and Practice Journal of Nizhny Novgorod Academy of the Ministry of Internal Affairs of Russia, 4*, 174–178.

Gheyas, I. A., & Abdallah, A. E. (2016). Detection and prediction of insider threats to cyber security: A systematic literature review and meta-analysis. *Big Data Analytics, 1*(1).

Gill, P. (2015). *Lone-Actor terrorists a behavioural analysis*. Routledge.

Granovetter, M. (1978). Threshold models of collective behavior. *American Journal of Sociology, 83*(6), 1420–1443.

Greenberg, J. (1990). Employee theft as a reaction to underpayment inequity: The hidden cost of pay cuts. *Journal of Applied Psychology, 75*(5), 561–568.

Greitzer, F. L., Kangas, L. J., Noonan, C. F., Brown, C. R., & Ferryman, T. (2013). Psychosocial modeling of insider threat risk based on behavioral and word use analysis. *E-Service Journal: A Journal of Electronic Services in the Public and Private Sectors, 9*(1), 106–138.

Greitzer, F.L., Kangas, L.J., Noonan, C.F., Dalton, A.C. and Hohimer, R.E. (2012). Identifying At-Risk Employees: Modeling Psychosocial Precursors of Potential Insider Threats. [online] IEEE Xplore. https://doi.org/10.1109/HICSS.2012.309.

Hare, R. D. (1999). Psychopathy as a risk factor for violence. *Psychiatric Quarterly, 70*(3), 181–197.

Holt, T. J. (2012). Exploring the intersections of technology, crime, and terror. *Terrorism and Political Violence, 24*(2), 337–354.

Hutchings, A., & Holt, T. J. (2015). A crime script analysis of the online stolen data market. *British Journal of Criminology, 55*(3), 596–614.

Martineau, M., Spiridon, E., & Aiken, M. (2023). A comprehensive framework for cyber behavioral analysis based on a systematic review of cyber profiling literature. *Forensic Sciences, 3*(3), 452–477.

Mitnick, K. D., & Simon, W. L. (2003). *The art of deception: Controlling the human element of security*. Wiley.

Karagiannopoulos, V. (2018). *Living with hacktivism: From conflict to symbiosis.* Palgrave Macmillan.
Kranenbarg, M. W., van Gelder, J.-L., Barends, A. J., & de Vries, R. E. (2022). Is there a cybercriminal personality? Comparing cyber offenders and offline offenders on HEXACO personality domains and their underlying facets. *Computers in Human Behavior, 140,* Article 107576.
Kshetri, N. (2010). *The global cybercrime industry: Economic, institutional and strategic perspectives.* Springer.
Naudts, L. (2019). Criminal profiling and non-discrimination: On firm grounds for the digital era? In: A. Vedder, J. Schroers, C. Ducuing & P. Valcke (Eds.), *Security and law. Legal and ethical aspects of public security, cyber security and critical infrastructure security* (pp. 63–96). Intersentia.
Padayachee, K. (2021). Joint effects of neutralisation techniques and the dark triad of personality traits on gender: An insider threat perspective. In *Conference on Information Communications Technology and Society (ICTAS)* (pp. 40–45).
Paulhus, D. L., & Williams, K. M. (2002). The dark triad of personality: Narcissism, machiavellianism and psychopathy. *Journal of Research in Personality, 36*(6), 556–563.
Raskin, R., & Terry, H. (1988). A principal-components analysis of the narcissistic personality inventory and further evidence of its construct validity. *Journal of Personality and Social Psychology, 54*(5), 890–902.
Romagna, M., & Leukfeldt, R. E. (2024). Becoming a hacktivist. Examining the motivations and the processes that prompt an individual to engage in hacktivism. *Journal of Crime and Justice, 47*(4), 1–19.
Sidanius, J. and Pratto, F. (1999). *Social dominance: An intergroup theory of social hierarchy and oppression.* Cambridge University Press.
Snook, B., Cullen, R. M., Bennell, C., Taylor, P. J., & Gendreau, P. (2008). The criminal profiling illusion: What's behind the smoke and mirrors? *Criminal Justice and Behavior, 35*(10), 1257–1276.
Solove, D. J. (2011). *Nothing to hide: The false tradeoff between privacy and security.* Yale University Press.
Turvey, B. E. (2011). *Criminal profiling: An introduction to behavioral evidence analysis.* Academic press.
Zuckerman, M. (1994). Impulsive unsocialized sensation seeking: The biological foundations of a basic dimension of personality. In *Temperament: Individual differences at the interface of biology and behavior* (pp. 219–255).

CHAPTER 7

Social Engineering and Manipulation

Abstract Social engineering continues to pose a significant threat by manipulating human psychology, thereby bypassing technical safeguards. Attackers exploit cognitive fallacies, including authority, trust, and reciprocity, to coerce individuals into disclosing sensitive data or granting unauthorised access. Social engineers can undermine rational judgement by combining deceptive strategies with emotional triggers, rendering even the most robust firewalls and encryption ineffective. This chapter investigates the distinction between persuasion and manipulation, illustrating how assailants employ common heuristics to develop persuasive tricks. It emphasises the constraints of technology-focused countermeasures by conducting an analysis of case studies and psychological research.

INTRODUCTION

Social engineering takes advantage of the very qualities that typically facilitate effective human interaction—trust, empathy, and the propensity to comply with perceived authority—to circumvent security systems without utilising technical exploits. Attackers exploit cognitive biases, such as the shortcuts individuals employ to make rapid decisions, to orchestrate ostensibly legitimate interactions that facilitate unauthorised access or data thievery by manipulating human cognition and behaviour. Social engineering presents a distinctive challenge in terms of detection

© The Author(s), under exclusive license to Springer Nature Switzerland AG 2025
T. Suslov, *Rethinking Security*, Crime Prevention and Security Management, https://doi.org/10.1007/978-3-031-92068-4_7

and prevention, as it is directed at the individual rather than the infrastructure, in contrast to strictly technical attacks. Victims may willingly disclose information that they would otherwise protect when they are influenced by urgency, credibility, or emotional indicators.

This chapter investigates the mechanisms of manipulation that are employed in social engineering, distinguishing them from ethical persuasion and demonstrating how malignant actors exploit organisational defences by leveraging human psychology. Based on research that identifies common biases, emotional triggers, and social signals, it illustrates why technology-centric strategies alone are insufficient to address contemporary security challenges. This chapter emphasises the potential of a more profound comprehension of manipulation to fortify defences and reduce the likelihood of social engineering breaches in corporate, governmental, and personal settings by deconstructing the strategies of assailants and emphasising the significance of comprehensive, human-centred interventions.

One of the most formidable security threats is social engineering, which exploits human psychology to circumvent technological security measures (Mitnick & Simon, 2003). Social engineering attacks, in contrast to conventional intrusions that depend on technical exploits, exploit human emotions, cognition, and trust to achieve unauthorised access, data exfiltration, or financial fraud (Hadnagy, 2018). Adversaries can circumvent robust technological defences and capitalise on inherent human tendencies, including trust, urgency, and obedience to authority, by employing manipulation rather than mere persuasion. It is essential to comprehend the mechanisms of manipulation in social engineering and the methods by which assailants select their victims in order to create effective countermeasures.

Manipulation and persuasion are occasionally used interchangeably; however, they differ in both ethical and practical aspects. Persuasion is a process in which individuals voluntarily alter their behaviour in response to rational arguments, and it is characterised by transparency and consent (Jacobs, 2020). Conversely, manipulation is coercive, deceptive, and exploitative, frequently exploiting human vulnerabilities to accomplish the attacker's objective (Handoko & Putri, 2019). Manipulation undermines the ethical principle of informed assent. In contrast to persuasive communication, which may still respect an individual's autonomy by providing factual information and allowing them to make a decision, manipulation frequently employs partial truths, emotive exploitation, or disguised motives. This opacity of ethical boundaries is precisely the reason why social engineering presents a significant obstacle to the security initiatives of both corporations and governments.

Cognitive conveniences that humans employ to make daily decisions are exploited by social engineers. These shortcuts, which are frequently referred to as heuristics, enable individuals to respond promptly to intricate stimuli; however, they also render them susceptible to deception (Tversky & Kahneman, 1974). For example, rational reasoning may be overridden by a sense of urgency that stresses the necessity of immediate action or the impending dire consequences. Authority is an additional influential variable. Milgram (1974) has shown that individuals are more likely to comply with requests from perceived authority figures in classic social psychology experiments. Attackers who impersonate high-ranking executives ("the CEO scam") or official agencies (e.g., tax authorities) can exploit this predisposition to achieve compliance.

Trust is equally important: attackers exploit this instinct by fabricating emails or digital communications that appear authentic, and many individuals are compelled to trust recognised brands, colleagues, or widely respected institutions (Nadeem et al., 2023).

Not all individuals are equally susceptible to social engineering assaults. The targets of attackers are meticulously chosen based on their hierarchical responsibilities, digital footprints, and cognitive biases. Social engineering attacks are generally classified into two categories: targeted (spear phishing and whaling) and mass phishing. Despite the fact that the majority of recipients will recognise the deception, a small percentage will inevitably fall victim to mass attacks, such as wide-scale phishing campaigns, which rely on pure volume. In contrast, targeted assaults concentrate on individuals who are of significant value (Pienta et al., 2020).

"Whaling" is a specialised form of spear phishing that is frequently employed by attackers to target senior personnel. Successful manipulation yields substantial profits due to the fact that these executives have the ability to authorise substantial financial transactions or grant extensive system access. Open-source intelligence (OSINT) techniques are employed by attackers to acquire information about potential victims, such as public records, job responsibilities, and social media activity (Bhusal, 2021). Despite the fact that high-profile targets receive more attention, general employees continue to be a common entry point. Even if executed crudely, widespread phishing campaigns capitalise on the likelihood of success: obtaining the credentials of a single user is frequently sufficient to establish a presence (Bhardwaj et al., 2020).

Attackers are able to manipulate victims into compromising security systems by exploiting fundamental aspects of human psychology in social engineering attacks. Social engineering, in contrast to strictly technical cyberattacks, employs cognitive fallacies, emotional triggers, and social influence to fool individuals into disclosing sensitive information, transferring funds, or granting unauthorised access. These psychological principles are profoundly ingrained in human cognition and behaviour, rendering them challenging to address solely through technological solutions.

One of the most effective techniques employed in social engineering is authority bias. Research in psychology has demonstrated that individuals are considerably more inclined to comply with requests when they regard the source as an authority figure, regardless of whether the request is unreasonable or detrimental (Milgram, 1974). The probability of critical inquiry is diminished by the psychological pressure to comply with authoritative commands and the perceived legitimacy of the request. The reciprocity principle further enhances the probability of compliance by capitalising on the inherent propensity of individuals to reciprocate favours. According to the theory of reciprocity, individuals are compelled to reciprocate when they receive something of value, regardless of whether it is tangible or psychological (Kolm, 2000). By providing minor favours, such as free software, exclusive reports, or personal assistance, social engineers create an implicit sense of indebtedness, thereby manipulating this bias.

Scarcity and urgency are additional cognitive fallacies that social engineers employ to obstruct rational thought and compel victims to act promptly. The scarcity principle, which was initially introduced in consumer psychology, elucidates why individuals regard restricted resources as more valuable and are more inclined to make impetuous decisions when confronted with limited availability (Tversky & Kahneman, 1974). Fraudulent warnings, such as emails that assert that a victim's account will be deactivated unless immediate action is taken, are employed by attackers to generate an artificial sense of urgency. This principle is also exploited by ransomware attacks, which impose countdown periods and require victims to pay before losing access to their encrypted files. Critical thinking is suppressed by the psychological tension caused by urgency, which renders victims more susceptible to manipulation.

Social engineers manipulate emotions to circumvent logical decision-making processes, in addition to cognitive biases. Attackers can compel victims to comply with requests that they would otherwise reject by inducing fear, panic, curiosity, avarice, empathy, or altruism. Fear and distress are among the most potent emotions that are exploited in social engineering attacks. The amygdala, a brain region responsible for emotional responses, is activated by fear, as demonstrated by neuroscience research (Šimić et al., 2021). This activates impaired rational thinking and increases susceptibility to external influence. Ransomware campaigns are heavily dependent on fear-based tactics, which involve menacing victims with permanent data loss unless a ransom is paid. Similarly, fraudulent messages that impersonate government agencies or financial institutions threaten recipients with account suspension or legal action, resulting in a high-pressure situation that encourages impetuous compliance.

Curiosity and avarice are additional psychological mechanisms that attackers employ to entice victims into opening malicious files or visiting compromised websites. Curiosity is a fundamental human characteristic that motivates individuals to pursue new information, even if it means exposing themselves to security risks (Litman, 2005). Greed exacerbates this effect by offering unrealistically lucrative employment opportunities, lottery winnings, or financial incentives.

Altruism and empathy are also exploited in social engineering attacks, as individuals are more inclined to concur with requests when they believe they are assisting someone in need. Psychological research has demonstrated that individuals are more inclined to act without verifying the legitimacy of the request when they are presented with emotionally compelling narratives, as evidenced by a heightened sense of obligation (Batson, 2011; Tomasello, 2020). This strategy is frequently employed in schemes that capitalise on humanitarian crises, medical emergencies, or natural disasters, where urgency and emotive appeal prevail over scepticism.

In ambiguous situations, social influence is a potent psychological force that significantly influences human behaviour. Social engineers manipulate victims into compliance by utilising social proof, commitment, and consistency. Social proof is the inclination to comply with the actions of others, particularly in ambiguous situations where individuals rely on external signals for guidance (Abdul Talib & Mat Saat, 2017). By fabricating testimonials, customer reviews, or false social media engagement, attackers exploit this principle to present fraudulent schemes as legitimate. In order to enhance the perceived legitimacy of their phishing campaigns, assailants may incorporate references to prominent industry figures or associates. Social proof is a psychological mechanism that explains why individuals are more inclined to engage in hazardous behaviour when they believe it has been validated by others.

The effectiveness of social engineering attacks is further enhanced by commitment and consistency, which capitalise on individuals' inclination to maintain consistency in their actions. The foot-in-the-door technique, a psychological strategy that has been extensively documented, entails the acquisition of a modest initial commitment before progressing to more substantial requests (Freedman & Fraser, 1966). In multi-stage phishing campaigns, attackers employ this approach by initially requesting that victims verify inconsequential details, such as their email address, before requesting more sensitive information. An individual is more inclined to concur with subsequent demands in order to preserve consistency in their behaviour after they have committed to an initial request.

Conclusion

Social engineering is a significant security concern due to its ability to exploit human vulnerabilities rather than solely technological deficiencies. Attackers can bypass even the most robust technical defences by deceiving individuals into divulging sensitive data or granting unauthorised access by exploiting trust, authority, urgency, and other cognitive biases. This manipulation is predicated on psychological principles that have been extensively studied, including authority bias, reciprocity, scarcity, and social proof. These principles have the potential to supersede rational judgement when the pressures of perceived legitimacy or dread are present.

The inference that should be derived is that effective countermeasures must encompass strategies that are focused on the human element and go beyond technical safeguards. Training programmes that improve situational awareness and critical thinking are essential for identifying suspicious requests and resisting emotional impulses. Additionally, organisations must cultivate a culture that prioritises security, encouraging employees to report anomalies rather than developing workarounds to cumbersome regulations. Furthermore, when implemented in conjunction with transparent leadership and consistent communication of best practices, adaptive policies that consider the social and psychological aspects of attacks can reduce risks.

Ultimately, security teams should endeavour to not only implement defensive technologies but also to provide individuals with the knowledge and resilience necessary to counter deceptive tactics. Organisations can establish a more comprehensive and effective defence against social engineering by recognising that human nature is a fundamental component of both the problem and the solution.

REFERENCES

Abdul Talib, Y. Y., & Mat Saat, R. (2017). Social proof in social media shopping: An experimental design research. *SHS Web of Conferences, 34*(02005), 02005.
Batson, C. D. (2011). *Altruism in Humans.* Oxford University Press.
Bhusal, C. S. (2021). Systematic review on social engineering: Hacking by manipulating humans. *Journal of Information Security, 12*(01), 104–114.
Bhardwaj, A., Sapra, V., Kumar, A., Kumar, N., & Arthi, S. (2020). Why is phishing still successful? *Computer Fraud & Security, 9*, 15–19.
Freedman, J. L., & Fraser, S. C. (1966). Compliance without pressure: The foot-in-the-door technique. *Journal of Personality and Social Psychology, 4*(2), 195–202.
Hadnagy, C. (2018). *Social engineering: The science of human hacking.* Wiley.
Handoko, H., & Putri, D. (2019). *Threat language: Cognitive exploitation in social engineering.* Proceedings of the International Conference on Social Sciences, Humanities, Economics and Law.
Jacobs, N. (2020). Two ethical concerns about the use of persuasive technology for vulnerable people. *Bioethics, 34*(5), 519–526.
Kolm, S. C. (2000). The Theory of Reciprocity. In Gérard-Varet, L. A., Kolm, S. C., Ythier, J. M. (Eds.), *The Economics of Reciprocity, Giving and Altruism.* International Economic Association Series. Palgrave Macmillan.
Litman, J. A. (2005). Curiosity and the pleasures of learning: Wanting and liking new information. *Cognition and Emotion, 19*(6), 793–814.
Milgram, S. (1974). *Obedience to authority: An experimental view.* Harper & Row.
Mitnick, K., & Simon, W. (2003). *The art of deception: Controlling the human element of security.* Wiley Publishing.
Nadeem, M., Zahra, S. W., Abbasi, M. N., Arshad, A., Riaz, S., & Ahmed, W. (2023). Phishing attack, its detections and prevention techniques. *International Journal of Wireless Security & Network, 1*, 13–25.

Pienta, D., Thatcher, J. B., & Johnston, A. (2020). Protecting a whale in a sea of phish. *Journal of Information Technology, 35*(3), 214–231.

Šimić, G., Tkalčić, M., Vukić, V., Mulc, D., Španić, E., Šagud, M., Olucha-Bordonau, F. E., Vukšić, M. R., & Hof, P. (2021) Understanding emotions: Origins and roles of the Amygdala. *Biomolecules, 11*(6), 823.

Tomasello, M. (2020). The moral psychology of obligation. *Behavioral and Brain Sciences, 43*, Article e56.

Tversky, A., & Kahneman, D. (1974). Judgment under uncertainty: Heuristics and biases. *Science, 185*(4157), 1124–1131.

PART III

Criminology

CHAPTER 8

Criminal Behaviour

Abstract This chapter offers a multi-dimensional examination of criminal behaviour, connecting classical criminological theories with modern security challenges. Foundational frameworks such as Routine Activity Theory, Rational Choice Theory, and Strain Theory elucidate the mechanism by which crime is generated by situational opportunities, cost–benefit analyses, and socio-economic pressures. These insights remain pivotal for modern security contexts, including cybercrime and insider threats. The chapter also investigates the cognitive distortions, personality traits, and situational factors that influence the decisions of offenders. By integrating life-course criminology, it underscores the evolving trajectories of criminal careers.

INTRODUCTION

This Chapter delves into the multifaceted nature of criminal behaviour, combining classical criminological perspectives with contemporary security challenges. A robust framework for comprehending how individuals become motivated to offend, how they evaluate the risks and rewards of illicit acts, and how social or economic pressures can drive deviance is provided by traditional theories, including Routine Activity Theory, Rational Choice Theory, and Strain Theory. Although these theories were developed prior to the digital era, they continue to be highly pertinent for the examination of modern criminal activities, such as organised crime, insider threats, and cybercrime.

This chapter also investigates the situational and psychological dimensions that influence offending, emphasising the ways in which environmental factors, personality characteristics, and cognitive processes can either facilitate or impede criminal decisions. Furthermore, it recognises the importance of life-course criminology in elucidating the process by which individuals transition from minor rule violations to significant criminal offences. The chapter provides a comprehensive approach for security professionals, policymakers, and researchers who are interested in the development of effective crime prevention and intervention strategies that are responsive to both individual and contextual determinants of criminal behaviour. This is achieved by integrating theoretical foundations with practical examples.

In contemporary security environments, a comprehension of classical criminological theories remains a critical foundation for the interpretation, prediction, and mitigation of criminal actions. Despite the fact that these theories were developed in historical contexts that predate the development of advanced digital technologies, their fundamental principles can be effectively adapted to address contemporary challenges, such as organised criminal networks, insider threats, and cybercrime. Security professionals and researchers can gain structured insights into the selection of targets and the justification of actions within organisational, cyber, and broader social environments by investigating Routine Activity Theory, Rational Choice Theory, and Strain Theory.

Routine Activity Theory, which was developed by Cohen and Felson (1979), asserts that crime occurs when three elements converge: the absence of capable guardianship, a motivated offender, and a suitable target. This theory underscores that criminal activity is not necessarily motivated by a deep-seated criminal intent, but rather by opportunities that arise in daily life. Routine Activity Theory explains how criminals exploit deficiencies in protective measures to carry out attacks when applied to security and cybercrime.

Inadequate monitoring of privileged accounts, a lack of encryption, or ineffectual access controls are all examples of weak security policies that reduce guardianship and create conditions in which security violations can occur with minimal risk. Williams et al. (2018) conducted a study on insider business cybercrime victimisation and discovered that organisations with inadequate internal controls encountered significantly higher rates of data breaches and fraud. Routine Activity Theory emphasises the detrimental effects of online anonymity on capable guardianship, rendering digital spaces more appealing to criminals in the context of cybercrime. For instance, cybercriminals are able to operate with minimal risk of detection by exploiting human error and lax security policies in phishing schemes and ransomware attacks.

Rational Choice Theory, which was devised by Cornish and Clarke (1986), posits that offenders are rational decision-makers who evaluate the advantages and disadvantages of committing a crime. This theory presupposes that perpetrators conduct a cost–benefit analysis to determine whether the prospective benefits of their actions outweigh the risks of apprehension and punishment. Rational Choice Theory elucidates the rationale behind the calculated decisions that cybercriminals and internal threats make when they target organisations in security contexts. Ransomware attacks and financial fraud are highly appealing to cybercriminals due to their low perceived risks and high rewards. The cost–benefit balance is further skewed in favour of offenders by the anonymity of cryptocurrency transactions, decentralised finance, and the dark web, which reduces the likelihood of law enforcement intervention (Gamel, 2025).

The Strain Theory, which was introduced by Robert Merton (1938), posits that criminal activity occurs when individuals are unable to attain socially acceptable objectives through legitimate means, resulting in emotional strain or pressure. This theory emphasises the potential for economic hardship, employment dissatisfaction, and social inequality to induce illicit behaviour in individuals, particularly in corporate and organisational environments. Strain Theory has been increasingly employed to elucidate cybercrime and internal threats, in addition to its traditional application in the analysis of street crime and financial fraud (Dearden et al., 2021). Strain Theory elucidates the reasons why employees who experience professional stagnation, underpayment, or mistreatment may resort to financial deception, data breaches, or sabotage in the context of insider threats.

Criminological theories provide comprehensive explanations for the reasons why individuals participate in illicit activities; however, the specific situational, psychological, and environmental factors that influence their behaviour and timing are the determining factors. In the context of security threats such as cybercrime, insider attacks, and corporate fraud, these influences shape offender behaviour by dictating decision-making patterns, reinforcing illicit motivations, and producing opportunities.

The immediate opportunities and environmental indicators that facilitate or impede illicit behaviours are referred to as situational factors in criminology (Cohen & Felson, 1979). Clarke (1983) emphasises that crime is frequently the consequence of conditions such as inadequate access controls, negligent surveillance, and other "facilitators," rather than the sole outcome of ingrained personal dispositions. These situational stimuli can have a significant impact on an individual's decision to commit an offence, regardless of whether it occurs in the physical or digital domain.

Opportunity structures are particularly impactful in modern security contexts. Traditional forms of security threats may involve physical intrusion through poorly guarded entrances or neglected alarm systems, but parallel vulnerabilities exist in digital environments. In this regard, environmental signals in the digital realm can be as influential as neglecting to secure doors in a physical location. Therefore, situational factors don't merely provide a background to crime; they also act as a catalyst, combining with the personal characteristics and motivations of the offender to increase the risk and opportunity of illicit activity.

In security contexts, criminal behaviour is significantly influenced by personality traits, cognitive distortions, and affective states, in addition to situational influences. Narcissism, psychopathy, and impulsivity are personality traits that have been linked to an increased likelihood of disregarding social norms or breaking rules (Hare et al., 1991). For example, in the context of corporate fraud or cybercrime, narcissistic personalities may perceive themselves as exempt from regulation, justifying their exploitation of systems or data as a self-serving act of ingenuity.

Cognitive distortions are instrumental in the facilitation of illicit decision-making by enabling individuals to rationalise their unethical actions (Maruna & Mann, 2006). These rationalisations allow individuals to participate in illicit activities without experiencing cognitive dissonance or remorse. It is imperative to comprehend these cognitive processes in order to create interventions that challenge and rectify distorted thinking patterns, thereby decreasing the probability of criminal behaviour.

Individuals may be motivated to engage in illicit activities by emotional states such as resentment, apathy, and thrill-seeking. As a form of retribution, an employee who is feeling unappreciated or resentful as a result of perceived injustices at work may indulge in data intrusions or sabotage. In contrast, individuals who are in search of exhilaration may resort to cybervandalism or hacking in order to satisfy their craving for stimulation. It is essential for organisations that want to establish work environments that resolve employee grievances and provide healthy outlets for tension and boredom to acknowledge the influence of these emotional states. This approach can help mitigate potential security threats.

Long-term participation in deviant activities or opportunistic responses to specific circumstances frequently influence criminal behaviour. Life-course criminology differentiates between career criminals, who engage in persistent and evolving criminal behaviour, and opportunistic offenders, who perpetrate crimes when the circumstances permit (Laub & Sampson, 2001). This distinction is evident in the progression of criminal careers in cybersecurity, where individuals progress from minor infractions (e.g., password sharing, unauthorised access) to large-scale offences (e.g., data exfiltration, ransomware operations). This transition is illustrated by the case of Kevin Mitnick (Mitnick & Simon, 2011), who began his career as a low-level hacker who engaged in social engineering attacks and phone phreaking. The role of peer validation and skill development in cybercriminal careers was demonstrated by the escalation of his offences into corporate espionage, unauthorised data access, and large-scale cyber intrusions. Intervention necessitates the identification of early warning indicators of security violations. An individual's transition towards illicit behaviour may be indicated by behavioural indicators such as abrupt changes in online activity, attempts to access restricted data, or inexplicable financial pressures.

Conclusion

The chapter emphasises that classical criminological theories, Routine Activity and Strain Theory, continue to possess significant explanatory value in contemporary security contexts, such as insider and cyber threats. These theories elucidate the pathways that lead individuals to offend by demonstrating how motivated offenders exploit inadequate guardianship, favourable cost–benefit ratios, or personal grievances. However, the chapter also emphasises that situational factors, personality traits, cognitive distortions, and emotional motivations all play equally significant roles in the formation of criminal decisions.

Ultimately, the convergence of theoretical perspectives offers a nuanced comprehension of criminal behaviour that surpasses mere opportunity. In order to prevent offences, including digital intrusions, fraud, and sabotage, organisations must combine environmental safeguards with continuous evaluations of human factors. The necessity of adaptive, multifaceted prevention strategies is further emphasised by the recognition that some offenders progressively establish a "criminal career" while others are influenced by opportunistic impulses. Security professionals and researchers can more effectively identify early warning signs, tailor responses, and curtail both isolated incidents and entrenched patterns of criminal conduct by balancing situational crime prevention measures with interventions that address personal, emotional, and social triggers.

References

Clarke, R. V. (1983). Situational crime prevention: Its theoretical basis and practical scope. *Crime and Justice, 4*(1), 225–256.

Cohen, L. E., & Felson, M. (1979). Social change and crime rate trends: A routine activity approach. *American Sociological Review, 44*(4).

Cornish, D., & Clarke, R. V. (1986). *The reasoning criminal: rational choice perspectives on offending.* Springer-Verlag.

Dearden, T. E., Parti, K., & Hawdon, J. (2021). Institutional anomie theory and cybercrime—Cybercrime and the American Dream. *Journal of Contemporary Criminal Justice, 37*(3), 311–332.

Gamel, M. (2025). Cryptocurrencies and the dark web: A gateway to money laundering. *Studies in Computational Intelligence,* 217–247.

Hare, R. D., Hart, S. D., & Harpur, T. J. (1991). Psychopathy and the DSM-IV criteria for antisocial personality disorder. *Journal of Abnormal Psychology, 100*(3), 391–398.

Laub, J. H., & Sampson, R. J. (2001). Understanding desistance from crime. *Crime and Justice, 28*(28), 1–69.

Maruna, S., & Mann, R. E. (2006). A fundamental attribution error? Rethinking cognitive distortions. *Legal and Criminological Psychology, 11*(2), 155–177.

Merton, R. K. (1938). Social structure and anomie. *American Sociological Review, 3*(5), 672–682.

Mitnick, K. D., & Simon, W. L. (2011). *The art of deception: controlling the human element of security.* Wiley.

Williams, M. L., Levi, M., Burnap, P., & Gundur, R. V. (2018). Under the corporate radar: Examining insider business cybercrime victimization through an application of routine activities theory. *Deviant Behavior, 40*(9), 1119–1131.

CHAPTER 9

Crime Prevention

Abstract This chapter explores a broad range of crime prevention strategies rooted in criminological theories that reduce criminal opportunities and address offender motivations. The chapter illustrates the efficacy of modifying ambient conditions to deter crime by examining Situational Crime Prevention, Defensible Space Theory, Routine Activity Modification, and Crime Prevention Through Environmental Design. These measures are designed to manage access in both physical and digital domains, encourage natural surveillance, and modify situational factors. While acknowledging broader structural influences, it emphasises the impact of cultural attitudes, norms, and nudges on security behaviours, with a particular emphasis on social psychology. Ultimately, a comprehensive strategy that integrates environmental, behavioural, and organisational interventions is the most effective method for long-term risk reduction and sustainable crime deterrence.

Introduction

The chapter explores a variety of crime prevention strategies that are based on fundamental criminological theories and are designed to mitigate criminal opportunities and address the motivations of offenders. These theories are the foundation for proactive measures that deter crime at its source in contemporary security management, which encompasses cybersecurity, corporate security, and physical security. This chapter demonstrates how the environment and human behaviour can be manipulated to reduce the feasibility or appeal of crime by examining frameworks such as Situational Crime Prevention (SCP), Defensible Space Theory (DST), and Routine Activity Modification (RAM).

Additionally, it integrates insights from Crime Prevention Through Environmental Design (CPTED), which prioritises the development of physical and digital domains to deter illicit activities by means of visibility, access control, and territoriality. The chapter also investigates the influence of psychological and social dynamics, including normative pressures, peer influence, and the role of nudges, on security behaviours, recognising the significance of human factors.

In general, the chapter offers a comprehensive perspective on crime prevention, illustrating that effective security strategies encompass environmental, behavioural, and organisational interventions that are meticulously orchestrated to achieve long-term crime deterrence, in addition to reactionary methods.

Many crime prevention strategies are based on criminological theories that are designed to decrease the number of criminal opportunities and to reduce the motivations of offenders. These theories inform proactive measures that deter crime before it occurs in the field of security management, particularly cybersecurity and physical security. Three noteworthy crime prevention frameworks—Situational Crime Prevention, Routine Activity Modification, and Defensible Space Theory—function as fundamental approaches to crime prevention in contemporary security contexts. These theories underscore the importance of modifying human behaviours and modifying environmental conditions to reduce the appeal or feasibility of crimes.

Situational Crime Prevention (SCP) is predicated on the notion that crime arises when there is a discernible opportunity, and that the reduction of such opportunities results in a decrease in offending (Clarke, 1997). SCP is distinguished from theories that concentrate on broad social factors by its emphasis on the immediate, situational circumstances that make criminal acts possible. The theoretical framework of SCP is structured around strategies that include enhancing the effort required to commit an offence (through enhanced locks or encryption measures), increasing the risk of detection (through surveillance systems), reducing the rewards associated with crime (by restricting access to valuable assets), removing provocations, and denying excuses. SCP prioritises the modification of the environment and the enhancement of the difficulty of perpetrating crimes through target fortification, enhanced surveillance, and security policies (Back & LaPrade, 2020).

Modern security contexts provide a multifaceted application for SCP. The notion of increasing the effort and risks for potential perpetrators is directly aligned with the use of stringent authentication mechanisms and network monitoring tools in digital environments. Physical security measures, including the installation of CCTV in parking areas and the implementation of rigorous access controls in offices, are parallel interventions that are designed to restrict the ease of larceny or unauthorised entry (Gill & Spriggs, 2005). These crime prevention measures underscore the fact that a more effective strategy for crime reduction in security management is to reduce opportunities, rather than solely focussing on apprehension and punishment (Nagin, 2013).

Defensible Space Theory, which was devised by Newman (1972), posits that crime can be deterred by creating environments that promote territoriality, natural surveillance, and access control. The theory suggests that the presence of physical and psychological barriers can serve to decrease crime by increasing the probability of detection and signalling ownership. Defensible Space Theory is seeing an increase in its application to smart city initiatives, cybersecurity, and corporate security, despite its origins in urban planning and public housing. The development of workplace security policies that designate responsibility for security awareness and conformance to employees is informed by Defensible Space Theory in the context of corporate security.

Research suggests that organisations that implement physical security design, including monitored workspaces, controlled access zones, and secured entry points, experience reduced rates of security breaches and insider threats (Radosteva, 2020). In contrast, natural surveillance entails the creation of environments that facilitate the observation of common areas by legitimate users, thereby elevating the perceived risk for criminals (Cozens et al., 2005). The value of designing spaces (including virtual ones) that signal vigilance is underscored by the adaptation of DST to integrated physical and digital security strategies, thereby dissuading those contemplating criminal acts.

The Routine Activity Theory, which was developed by Cohen and Felson (1979), is the foundation of Routine Activity Modification. This theory asserts that crime is more likely to occur when three elements converge in time and space: a motivated offender, a suitable target, and the absence of capable guardianship. Organisations can substantially mitigate security risks by modifying behaviours and instituting security practices that disrupt crime-prone situations. Routine Activity Modification has also been implemented in the context of employee awareness training and digital hygiene practices. These practices encompass periodic security training, phishing awareness campaigns, and behavioural reinforcement strategies. Research indicates that organisations that implement robust security training programmes experience substantially reduced cybercrime incidents, as employees become less susceptible to phishing schemes and social engineering tactics (Kikerpill, 2020).

Crime Prevention Through Environmental Design (CPTED) is a security strategy that emphasises the development of physical and digital environments to mitigate the potential for criminal activity. CPTED, which was initially introduced by Ray Jeffery (1971) and subsequently developed by Oscar Newman (1972), is predicated on the idea that well-designed spaces can inadvertently discourage criminal behaviour by enhancing visibility, establishing territorial ownership, and limiting unauthorised access. The theory is extensively utilised in the fields of urban planning, corporate security, cybersecurity, and smart city infrastructure, where strategic design decisions are made to mitigate security threats. The fundamental principles of CPTED are centred on the modification of the built environment to reduce the likelihood of crime. These principles have been extensively investigated and implemented in a variety of security and crime prevention strategies, such as corporate security, urban development, and cybersecurity (Armitage, 2016).

Natural surveillance is one of the most critical principles of CPTED, as it is designed to enhance visibility in an environment in order to discourage criminal activity. This principle is predicated on the notion that criminals are less inclined to commit crimes in areas where they perceive that they are being monitored. Research suggests that crime rates are lower in areas with effective illumination and open sightlines, as perpetrators perceive a greater likelihood of being observed and apprehended (Armitage et al., 2018). Access control is another fundamental CPTED principle that entails the restriction of entry to specific areas in order to mitigate unauthorised activities. Fences, gates, and secure entry systems are utilised in residential and commercial areas to establish boundaries and regulate movement, thereby restricting the potential for criminal intrusion.

Territorial reinforcement is a concept that emphasises the establishment of a distinct sense of ownership over spaces in order to deter criminal activity and unauthorised access. This principle is especially effective in corporate environments, where security measures such as branded office spaces, employee-only areas, and ID badges reinforce a controlled environment. In urban planning strategies, territoriality is also apparent, as public spaces are designed to discourage illicit behaviours and promote legitimate use (Shirazi et al., 2021).

A final critical CPTED principle is maintenance and image, which pertains to the preservation of physical environments in order to prevent criminal activity. This principle is closely aligned with the Broken Windows Theory (Kelling & Wilson, 1982), which posits that visible indicators of disorder (e.g., vandalism, graffiti, and unkempt areas) contribute to criminal activity. Research has demonstrated that well-maintained spaces promote a sense of community responsibility and deter crime, as offenders perceive a greater likelihood of detection and intervention.

In the context of office design, illumination, and controlled entry points, physical security has been the primary focus of CPTED applications for a long time. Atlas (2013) observes that the strategic placement of illumination can significantly alter the offender's perspective, rendering it more difficult to remain undetected while attempting to commit a break-in or other illegal activity. These architectural choices are further enhanced by access control systems, which establish a stratified defence mechanism that can range from key card entry for general areas to biometric identification for highly restricted zones (Crowe, 2000). Collectively, these measures reinforce the perception that an area is closely managed while simultaneously mitigating potential vulnerabilities.

Scholars and practitioners are increasingly discussing "digital CPTED" as a conceptual extension of environmental design in cyberspace, despite the fact that CPTED is traditionally orientated towards physical design (Holt & Bossler, 2015). In practical terms, layered security protocols simulate natural surveillance and access control. Utilising environmental design, territorial reinforcement, access control, and maintenance to discourage criminal activity, CPTED continues to be one of the most effective crime prevention frameworks.

Criminal activity is not exclusively the result of environmental design deficiencies or situational opportunities. It is also influenced by the cognitive processes, affective states, social relationships, and broader structural factors of individuals. The recognition that individuals' decisions are rarely made in a vacuum is reflected in the application of cognitive and social psychology to crime prevention. Rather, they are significantly impacted by normative pressures, social signals, moral disengagement, and perceptions of risk and reward (Bandura, 1999). In organisational and workplace settings, employees frequently rely on the guidance of their colleagues and superiors to interpret company policies, assess acceptable levels of risk, and influence their daily activities, including those associated with security practices (Kraemer et al., 2009).

For example, employees are more likely to normalise these risky behaviours if an organisation's informal culture tolerates lax password sharing or only sporadically enforces data protection rules.

The influence of social norms on behaviour, particularly in ambiguous situations, is illustrated by a substantial body of empirical research (Cialdini & Trost, 1998). Not only do employees receive practical guidance on permissible conduct, but they also experience implicit social pressure to conform when they observe peers or superiors engaging in secure practices—such as consistently updating passwords, reporting suspicious emails, or adhering to restricted-access protocols.

Nudges, as they are defined in behavioural economics, are discreet reminders that encourage individuals to take desired actions without the use of direct mandates or overbearing enforcement (Thaler & Sunstein, 2008). Nudging techniques can be particularly effective in modern organisations for promoting secure behaviours by incorporating reminders or warnings at critical junctures. For instance, users may be advised to exercise caution by brief prompts regarding password complexity or the identification of recent phishing attempts on logon screens. In the same vein, automated system notifications can serve as a reminder to employees to secure their workstations when they are absent from their workspaces or to confirm the recipients of sensitive documents prior to transmitting them.

Additionally, it is important to consider the influence of emotion on the development of behavioural change. Scholars have demonstrated that fear appeals, although occasionally effective in the short term, may diminish in effectiveness over time or elicit maladaptive responses, such as avoidance or denial (Bada et al., 2019). A more constructive approach frequently entails celebrating compliance successes and positively framing security as a shared responsibility, such as awarding recognition to departments with the fewest policy violations.

It is equally essential to address the fundamental causes that motivate some individuals to engage in criminal conduct, despite the fact that shaping behaviour through social norms and nudges is crucial. Strain theories and related perspectives posit that individuals may be motivated to engage in illicit activities by economic pressures, workplace stress, and social inequalities, particularly if they perceive that there are few legitimate opportunities for advancement (Agnew, 2001). Therefore, a comprehensive crime prevention strategy must not only prevent opportunities but also address the stressors and grievances that predispose individuals to deviance.

Conclusion

This chapter emphasises the critical importance of proactive crime prevention strategies, which are founded on both human behavioural insights and environmental design. The deterrent effect of Situational Crime Prevention is more immediate than that of punitive approaches alone, as it demonstrates the potential to reduce criminal opportunities through enhanced surveillance, access controls, and target fortification. Routine Activity Modification concentrates on disrupting the convergence of motivated offenders, suitable targets, and inadequate guardianship, while Defensible Space Theory emphasises the significance of territory and natural surveillance in deterring unlawful activity.

Crime Prevention Through Environmental Design (CPTED) expands upon these principles by methodically reshaping physical and, increasingly, digital spaces to deter offenders through visibility, access control, and maintenance. Nevertheless, the efficacy of these frameworks is also contingent upon psychological and social factors. Cognitive and social psychology have demonstrated that security behaviours are significantly influenced by organisational cultures, social norms, and nudges, which can range from reminders to recognition programmes.

Finally, crime prevention is not limited to the mere removal of opportunities or the augmentation of risks. Organisations can cultivate a culture that not only discourages deviant behaviour but also encourages collective responsibility for security and risk management by balancing environmental modifications, robust policies, and a profound comprehension of human motivations.

REFERENCES

Agnew, R. (2001). Building on the Foundation of General Strain Theory: Specifying the Types of Strain Most Likely to Lead to Crime and Delinquency. *Journal of Research in Crime and Delinquency, 38*(4), 319–361.

Armitage, R. (2016). Crime prevention through environmental design. In Environmental criminology and crime analysis (pp. 278–304). Routledge.

Armitage, R., Joyce, C., & Monchuk, L. (2018). Crime Prevention Through Environmental Design (CPTED) and Retail Crime: Exploring Offender Perspectives on Risk and Protective Factors in the Design and Layout of Retail Environments. 123–154.

Atlas, R. I. (2013). *21st century security and CPTED : Designing for critical infrastructure protection and crime prevention*. Crc Press.

Back, S., & LaPrade, J. (2020). Cyber-Situational Crime Prevention and the Breadth of Cybercrimes among Higher Education Institutions. *International Journal of Cybersecurity Intelligence & Cybercrime, 3*(2), 25–47.

Bada, M., Sasse, A.M. and Nurse, J.R.C. (2019). Cyber Security Awareness Campaigns: Why do they fail to change behaviour?

Bandura, A. (1999). Social cognitive theory of personality. In L. A. Pervin & O. P. John (Eds.), *Handbook of personality: Theory and research* (2nd ed., pp. 154–196). Guilford Press.

Cialdini, R. B., & Trost, M. R. (1998). Social influence: Social norms, conformity and compliance. In D. T. Gilbert, S. T. Fiske, & G. Lindzey (Eds.), The handbook of social psychology 4th ed. McGraw-Hill. pp. 151–192.

Clarke, R. V. (1997). Situational crime prevention : successful case studies. Boulder, Colorado ; London: Lynne Rienner Publishers.

Cozens, P. M., Saville, G., & Hillier, D. (2005). Crime prevention through environmental design (CPTED): A review and modern bibliography. *Property Management, 23*(5), 328–356.

Crowe, T. (2000). *Crime Prevention Through Environmental Design*. Elsevier Science.

Gill, M., & Spriggs, A. (2005). *Assessing the impact of CCTV* (Vol. 292). Home Office Research, Development and Statistics Directorate.

Holt, T., & Bossler, A. (2015). Cybercrime in progress: Theory and prevention of technology-enabled offenses. Routledge.

Jeffery, C. R. (1971). Crime Prevention Through Environmental Design. *American Behavioral Scientist, 14*(4), 598–598.

Kelling, G. and Wilson, J. (1982) BROKEN WINDOWS The police and neighborhood safety. The Atlantic Monthly, pp. 1–12.

Kikerpill, K. (2020). The individual's role in cybercrime prevention: Internal spheres of protection and our ability to safeguard them. *Kybernetes, 50*, 1015–1026.

Kraemer, S., Carayon, P., & Clem, J. (2009). Human and organizational factors in computer and information security: Pathways to vulnerabilities. *Computers & Security, 28*(7), 509–520.

Nagin, D. (2013). Deterrence in the Twenty-First Century. *Crime and Justice, 42*(1), 199–263.

Newman, O. (1972). *Defensible Space; Crime Prevention through Urban Design.* Macmillan.

Radosteva, Y. V. (2020). To the Issue of Situational Crime Prevention. In XVII International Research-to-Practice Conference dedicated to the memory of MI Kovalyov. Atlantis Press. pp. 76–79.

Shirazi, E., Bidaki, R., Shirazi, S., Shalbafan, M. R., Sadri-Kermani, C., & Shafaat, A. B. (2021). Crime Prevention through Environmental Design (CPTED): Psychocognitive Effect of Appropriate Environmental Design on Preventing Criminal Behavior and Improving Social Security. *Journal of Rafsanjan University of Medical Sciences, 20*(2), 235–242.

Thaler, R. H., & Sunstein, C. R. (2008). *Nudge: Improving decisions about health, wealth, and happiness.* Yale University Press.

PART IV

New Approach

CHAPTER 10

Human-Centric Models and Behavioural Security

Abstract This chapter discusses the transition from hierarchical security models to human-centric, adaptable frameworks that are capable of addressing sophisticated threats. User disengagement is promoted by an excessive reliance on compliance-based measures, which in turn induces employees to implement hazardous remedies. In the interim, the importance of cross-sector collaboration is emphasised by the escalating international cyber threats. Behavioural-based security acknowledges that risks are primarily caused by human behaviour. An adaptive security culture is fostered by prioritising education, leadership, and positive reinforcement, which ultimately fortifies organisational resilience, engages stakeholders, and facilitates risk mitigation. A proactive approach to rapidly evolving threats is guaranteed by a collaborative model that incorporates interdepartmental coordination.

Keywords Collaborative security frameworks · Cross-department integration · Public–private partnerships · International cooperation · Behavioural security culture

Introduction

The subsequent chapter investigates the critical transition from conventional, hierarchical security models to more adaptive, human-centric frameworks that consider collaborative practices and behavioural dynamics. The assumption that robust technical controls can mitigate all risks is often the foundation of conventional strategies, which rely on centralised authority and rigorous rules. Nevertheless, these rigid systems have been surpassed by contemporary cyber threats, such as social engineering, which have exposed substantial deficiencies in compliance-based security strategies. Employees frequently develop workarounds or disdain protocols wholly when security measures are excessively restrictive, resulting in hazardous operational gaps.

This chapter posits that meaningful security improvements stem from recognising human behaviour as the root cause of most breaches, rather than focusing solely on technological defences. A more resilient model is established by incorporating insights from organisational theory and behavioural psychology, which prioritise proactive risk management, education, and collaboration. The necessity of unified endeavours to confront increasingly sophisticated attacks will be underscored through the examination of practical strategies for interdepartmental cooperation, public–private partnerships, and international alliances. Ultimately, this chapter demonstrates the importance of adopting human-centric approaches and flexible security cultures to establish an environment in which technology and behaviour align to fortify security defences.

Traditional security models are frequently hierarchical in nature, relying on a centralised authority to establish policies, enforce regulations, and govern access. This rigorous framework presupposes that security threats can be attenuated through the implementation of strict access controls, the enforcement of policies, and reactive threat management. Although this model has been historically effective in structured environments, such as corporate IT networks, it is not well-suited to the dynamic security landscape of today. Its primary weakness is its incapacity to adjust to the rapidly changing nature of security risks, particularly those that involve social engineering, decentralised networks, and zero-day vulnerabilities (Awodele et al., 2024; Sasi et al., 2023).

Gallagher et al. (2022) introduced the COLBAC (Collective-Based Access Control) framework, which underscores the operational inefficiencies and security gaps that rigid access controls frequently create in horizontally structured organisations, such as worker cooperatives and activist networks. This framework serves as a testament to the constraints of hierarchical security models. Real-time responses are required due to the increasing sophistication of intrusions, including AI-driven attacks and ransomware, which traditional structures are unable to provide (Zaid & Garai, 2024).

Moreover, research has demonstrated that employees devise workarounds to circumvent security controls that are excessively strict (Beautement et al., 2008; Kirlappos et al., 2015). This conduct not only compromises security but also underscores the necessity of adaptable, behaviourally informed security policies that incorporate human factors into security decision-making.

The overreliance on compliance-based security policies is another significant criticism of traditional security models. While compliance frameworks, including ISO 27001, NIST, and GDPR, are crucial for establishing baseline security standards, they frequently result in a checklist-based mentality that prioritises regulatory adherence over genuine security enhancements (Folorunso et al., 2024). User disengagement is a significant concern with compliance-driven security. Compliance requirements are frequently perceived as bureaucratic obligations by security professionals and employees, rather than as substantive security measures. Research indicates that employees are more inclined to implement security workarounds, including sharing passwords, circumventing authentication procedures, or deactivating security controls, when security policies are perceived as excessively restrictive or disconnected from daily operations (Ferreira et al., 2013).

The pressing necessity for a transition to adaptive, behaviourally-informed security frameworks is underscored by the shortcomings of conventional hierarchical security models. The rigid rule-based approach known as "Comply or die" (Kirlappos et al., 2013) is no longer adequate as security challenges become more complex and dynamic.

A new collaborative security model emphasises the importance of international collaboration, public–private partnerships, and cooperation among internal organisational departments, thereby cultivating a security environment that is more proactive, resilient, and adaptive. In the realm of contemporary security, rigorous enforcement models that prioritise compliance over engagement result in inefficiencies and impede the rapid response to risks. It is imperative to transition from "command and control" to communication and collaboration in order to guarantee that security strategies are inclusive and adaptable.

Incident response times and risk mitigation capabilities are enhanced by models that integrate interdepartmental collaboration (Oriola et al., 2021). This change acknowledges that security is not solely a technical issue, but also an organisational and societal challenge that necessitates shared responsibility among stakeholders. IT departments are not the sole entities responsible for security; rather, it must be incorporated into various business functions, such as executive leadership, risk management, and human resources (HRA). For instance, IT teams are accountable for the technical defence infrastructure; however, their endeavours are frequently undermined by human vulnerabilities, including vulnerability to phishing, inadequate password management, and social engineering attacks (Herath & Rao, 2009). HR departments are essential in the prevention of internal threats and the preservation of security-conscious workplace cultures, as they are responsible for security training, awareness, and employee monitoring (Warkentin and Willison, 2009).

Public–private partnerships are indispensable for the development of security resilience, in addition to internal collaboration. It is imperative that governments and private corporations collaborate to develop joint security frameworks, share threat intelligence, and coordinate cyber incident responses. Tropina (2015)'s research indicates that cybersecurity hazards are ineffectively managed in isolation, as they frequently exceed national and organisational boundaries. Nevertheless, effective collaboration is impeded by information asymmetry and a lack of trust between governments and corporations. Tropina (2015) emphasises that the enhancement of public–private cybersecurity cooperation necessitates the implementation of mandatory security incident reporting, standardised security protocols, and real-time intelligence sharing. Although these regulatory initiatives have improved accountability and transparency, they must be supplemented by voluntary, trust-based collaboration to guarantee a proactive and collaborative security approach.

The significance of international cooperation in security has grown as threats have surpassed national borders. State-sponsored cyber espionage, human trafficking, cyberattacks, and terrorism have a significant impact on numerous jurisdictions, necessitating the establishment of bilateral and multilateral security alliances. Kosseff (2018)'s research emphasises that a fragmented approach to global cybersecurity governance results in inconsistencies in security policies, weakened defence mechanisms, and increased vulnerabilities.

Global alliances, which can be established through treaties, conventions, or intergovernmental organisations, can offer technical expertise, cross-border investigative powers, and shared legal frameworks. The potential for effective international collaboration is demonstrated by initiatives such as the EU-US Working Group on Cybersecurity and Cybercrime. Nevertheless, cybersecurity diplomacy is frequently impeded by geopolitical tensions and conflicting national interests. The challenges of sustaining cyber agreements between rival nations are underscored by a study conducted by Purwanti (2020) on US–China cybersecurity cooperation. International cooperation continues to be one of the most effective strategies for ensuring a stable digital environment and combating cyber threats, despite these challenges.

Technological innovation, policy coordination, and behavioural security strategies must be incorporated into a novel collaborative security model. By transitioning from inflexible enforcement mechanisms to dynamic, cooperative security frameworks, organisations, governments, and international stakeholders will be able to more effectively address newly emergent risks.

Security risks are fundamentally rooted in human behaviour rather than technology itself. While technological tools serve as critical enablers for cybersecurity, they are not the primary cause of security failures. Rather, the primary factor in security breaches is the human behaviour, whether through negligence, ignorance, or malicious intent (Hadnagy, 2018; Kadena & Gupi, 2021). The pressing necessity to transition from reactive, technology-centric security models to proactive, behaviour-based strategies that address the underlying causes of security risks is underscored by the growing complexity of cyber threats.

The erroneous belief that security is predominantly a technological issue has resulted in numerous organisations prioritising the pursuit of evolving technology over the mitigation of the behavioural fundamental causes of security risks (Sasse et al., 2001). Organisations frequently develop an illusory sense of security as a result of their growing dependence on security technology, as they assume that investments in firewalls, intrusion detection systems, and artificial intelligence will mitigate security risks. Nevertheless, research indicates that even the most sophisticated security systems can be circumvented if human users neglect to identify risks or adhere to inadequate security protocols (Beautement et al., 2008).

Behavioural patterns, decision-making biases, and a lack of security awareness are the underlying causes of security failures, rather than the constraints of technology. A change in organisational security culture is necessary to address security as a behavioural issue rather than a purely technological challenge. The cultivation of a security-conscious mindset extends beyond mere conformance by encouraging personal responsibility, critical thinking, and active engagement in security practices. In lieu of implementing punitive and restrictive security policies, organisations should prioritise the promotion of security-conscious behaviours through behavioural design, education, and positive reinforcement (Herley, 2009; Thaler & Sunstein, 2008).

Security culture is not established through a single training session or compliance checklist; rather, it is developed through ongoing engagement, leadership support, and integration into organisational values (Schlienger & Teufel, 2003). Leadership is essential in establishing the tone for security culture, as employees are more inclined to embrace security-conscious behaviours when they observe their leaders actively prioritising security (Willie, 2023).

This necessitates a reevaluation of the manner in which security is communicated, transitioning from fear-based messaging regarding cyber threats to the empowerment of individuals with practical security knowledge that can be applied in both their personal and professional lives (Adams & Sasse, 1999). Organisations must acknowledge that security is fundamentally a behavioural challenge, and sustainable enhancements can only be realised through a human-centred approach that emphasises psychological resilience, education, and security-conscious decision-making as risks continue to evolve.

Conclusion

Security education is no longer a supplementary component of IT security; it is now a fundamental component of organisational resilience. The evolving landscape of the security risks is not adequately addressed by traditional hierarchical security models, which are predicated on reactive policies and restrictive access controls. The growing sophistication of attacks, particularly those that exploit human vulnerabilities such as phishing and social engineering, proves that compliance-driven security policies are insufficient. The necessity for a security model that is human-centric and behaviourally informed is underscored by the fact that employees frequently ignore excessively restrictive controls. This model should incorporate adaptive learning, collaboration, and flexibility.

A transition from restrictive enforcement mechanisms to a collaborative security model promotes increased engagement and agility. Threat mitigation is improved through interdepartmental collaboration among IT, HR, and risk management teams. To mitigate cross-border cyber threats, public–private partnerships and international security cooperation are indispensable. Security cannot be restricted to IT departments; it must be integrated into the organisation's structure to guarantee that employees at all levels actively participate in risk mitigation.

In essence, security risks are a result of human behaviour, rather than technological constraints. Education, awareness, and psychological resilience are the primary objectives of a behavioural security approach. In place of punitive, fear-driven security policies, organisations should promote habit formation by fostering a security culture that is driven by leadership, personalised interventions, and positive reinforcement. An adaptive training programme, in conjunction with a security-conscious workforce, will be more effective in identifying and responding to risks than any standalone technological solution. The future of security is contingent upon the integration of behavioural science with security strategy, which will transform security into a shared responsibility rather than an imposed burden.

REFERENCES

Adams, A., & Sasse, M. A. (1999). Users are not the enemy. *Communications of the ACM*, *42*(12), 40–46 [online].

Awodele, O., Ogbonna, C., Ogu, E. O., Hinmikaiye, J. O., & Akinsola, J. E. T. (2024). Characterization and risk assessment of cyber security threats in cloud computing: A comparative evaluation of mitigation techniques. *Acadlore Transactions on AI and Machine Learning*, *3*(2), 106–118 [online].

Beautement, A., Sasse, M. A., & Wonham, M. (2008). The compliance budget: Managing security behaviour in organisations. In *Proceedings of the 2008 Workshop on New Security Paradigms* (pp. 47–58).

Ferreira, A., Correia, R., Chadwick, D., Santos, H. M. D., Gomes, R., Reis, D., & Antunes, L. (2013). *Password sharing and how to reduce it* (pp. 22–42). IGI Global eBooks.

Folorunso, A., Wada, I., Samuel, B., & Mohammed, V. (2024). Security compliance and its implication for cybersecurity. *World Journal of Advanced Research and Reviews*, *24*(1), 2105–2121 [online].

Gallagher, K., Torres-Arias, S., Memon, N., & Feldman, J. (2022). COLBAC: Shifting cybersecurity from hierarchical to horizontal designs. In *Proceedings of the 2021 New Security Paradigms Workshop (NSPW'21)* (pp. 13–27). Association for Computing Machinery, New York, NY, USA.

Hadnagy, C. (2018). *Social engineering*. Wiley Publishing, Inc. [online].

Herath, T., & Rao, H. R. (2009). Protection motivation and deterrence: A framework for security policy compliance in organisations. *European Journal of Information Systems, 18*(2), 106–125.

Herley, C. (2009). So long, and no thanks for the externalities. In *Proceedings of the 2009 Workshop on New Security Paradigms Workshop*.

Kadena, E., & Gupi, M. (2021). Human factors in cybersecurity. *Security Science Journal, 2*(2), 51–64.

Kirlappos, I., Beautement, A., & Sasse, M. A. (2013). "Comply or die" is dead: Long live security-aware principal agents. In A. A. Adams, M. Brenner, & M. Smith (Eds.), *Financial cryptography and data security*. FC 2013. Lecture Notes in Computer Science (Vol. 7862). Springer.

Kirlappos, I., Parkin, S., & Sasse, M. A. (2015). 'Shadow security' as a tool for the learning organization. *ACM SIGCAS Computers and Society, 45*(1), 29–37.

Kosseff, J. (2018). Defining cybersecurity law. *Iowa Law Review, 103*(3), 985–1031 [online].

Oriola, O., Adeyemo, A. B., Papadaki, M., & Kotzé, E. (2021). A collaborative approach for national cybersecurity incident management. *Information & Computer Security, 29*(3), 457–484.

Purwanti, D. (2020). The United States motivation in having cyber security cooperation with China. *Journal of International Studies on Energy Affairs, 2*(1), 105–122.

Sasi, T., Lashkari, A. H., Lu, R., Xiong, P., & Iqbal, S. (2023). A comprehensive survey on IoT attacks: Taxonomy, detection mechanisms and challenges. *Journal of Information and Intelligence, 2*(6).

Sasse, M. A., Brostoff, S., & Weirich, D. (2001). Transforming the 'weakest link'—A human/computer interaction approach to usable and effective security. *BT Technology Journal, 19*(3), 122–131 [online].

Schlienger, T., & Teufel, S. (2003). Information security culture—From analysis to change. *South African Computer Journal, 31*, 46–52.

Thaler, R. H., & Sunstein, C. R. (2008). *Nudge: Improving decisions about health, wealth, and happiness*. Yale University Press.

Tropina, T. (2015). *Public–private collaboration: Cybercrime, cybersecurity and national security* (pp. 1–41). SpringerBriefs in Cybersecurity.

Warkentin, M., & Willison, R. (2009). Behavioral and policy issues in information systems security: The insider threat. *European Journal of Information Systems, 18*(2), 101–105.

Willie, M. M. (2023). The role of organizational culture in cybersecurity: Building a security-first culture. *Journal of Research, Innovation and Technologies, II*(2(4)), 179–198 [online].

Zaid, T., & Garai, S. (2024). Emerging trends in cybersecurity: A holistic view on current threats, assessing solutions, and pioneering new frontiers. *Blockchain in Healthcare Today, 7*(1) [online].

CHAPTER 11

Security Education

Abstract Within today's modern organisations, security education is an absolute need since technical measures cannot, on their own, prevent breaches that are caused by human. This chapter examines why traditional training methods often fail, citing rote learning, compliance-driven approaches, and security fatigue as key culprits. Instead, research has shown that strategies that are dynamic and rich in context, such as emotional involvement, scenario-based learning, and spaced repetition, are effective in improving memory retention and situational awareness. When it comes to the formation of secure habits, cognitive and behavioural theories emphasise the significance of problem-solving, peer role models, and positive reinforcement. By using BJ Fogg's Behaviour Model and incorporating habit formation into everyday routines, organisations have the ability to construct a security culture that is both resilient and proactive, allowing them to adapt to the ever-changing nature of security risks.

Keywords Psychology-based training · Gamification of learning · Scenario-based exercises · Interdisciplinary collaboration · Empowerment and resilience

Introduction

The education of security personnel is an essential component of modern organisations, particularly in light of the fact that cyber threats are becoming more complex and sophisticated. In spite of the fact that firewalls, encryption, and intrusion detection systems are all essential technological precautions, the final success of these defences is dependent on the activities of humans. Because of this, organisations can no longer depend exclusively on policies that are motivated by compliance in order to reduce risks by themselves. It is instead necessary for them to build a culture that is security-conscious, one in which employees are provided with the information and incentive necessary to defend against dangers that are always growing.

A greater number of people are working remotely, cloud infrastructures are becoming more widespread, and the Internet of Things (IoT) has increased the potential attack surface. Due to the nature of the environment, it is not reasonable to believe that the whole duty for the protection of digital assets is with the information technology departments. Each and every person who has access to company networks or data has the potential to unintentionally "open a door" for cybercriminals. In light of this, security education need to be incorporated into each and every function, ranging from human resources and finance to marketing and senior leadership.

The reasons why traditional security training frequently fails are discussed in this chapter, as well as the ways in which organisations might adopt a model that is more successful and learner-centric. The chapter shows the significance of utilising psychological theories of learning and habit formation in order to reinforce safe behaviours. This is accomplished by analysing cutting-edge educational tactics such as spaced repetition, scenario-based training, and emotional involvement. Ultimately, the objective is to change security from a compliance-driven, top-down exercise into a comprehensive enterprise-wide duty that gives employees the ability to actively protect important resources.

Because of the ever-increasing complexity and level of sophistication of cyber threats, security education has become an essential component of modern organisations. While previous security techniques have mostly concentrated on technological defences, firewalls, and access restrictions, it is important to note that the effectiveness of these measures is only as effective as the individuals interacting with them. Errors made by humans continue to be the most common reason for security breaches. It is possible for even the most sophisticated security measures to be made useless if the appropriate education and awareness are not provided.

According to Kadena and Gupi (2021), technology solutions such as firewalls, encryption, and intrusion detection systems continue to be vital; nevertheless, these solutions are not adequate on their own to mitigate human-related security risks. Human mistake is responsible for the great majority of security breaches, according to studies that have been conducted repeatedly (Hughes-Lartey et al., 2021). Rather than relying merely on compliance-driven policies, this emphasises the critical need for organisations to shift their attention towards security education. Companies should make it a priority to ensure that personnel at all levels adopt a security-conscious mentality.

There has been an expansion in the attack surface for cybercriminals as a result of the rising interconnection of global commercial activities. The Internet of Things (IoT), cloud-based infrastructures, and remote work have all contributed to an increase in the number of possible vulnerabilities. As a result, it is essential for employees to be aware of the significance of implementing secure practices in their day-to-day operations (Dimitrov, 2020; Sasi et al., 2023).

Despite the fact that every person who has access to an organisation's network or data might serve as an entry point for attackers, traditional top-down, IT-driven security approaches frequently make the assumption that IT departments are the only ones responsible for cybersecurity. Therefore, security education has to expand beyond IT teams and become ingrained in the larger business culture. It should place an emphasis on security literacy across all departments (human resources, finance, marketing, and senior leadership), including executive leadership.

In this way, the significance of security education in contemporary organisations extends beyond the restricted purpose of teaching technical skills to employees. Not only does it ensure that individuals develop task-specific competences, but it also ensures that they develop an overall feeling of responsibility. This is where its genuine worth lies: in the fact that it places security-conscious thinking across the whole organisational structure. Through this approach, businesses are able to develop communities of employees that are both adaptable and engaged, so enhancing their ability to anticipate and respond to dangers more effectively than any technological solution that is implemented in isolation. The foundation of an organisation's resilience in this day and age, when breaches are increasingly exploiting human weaknesses rather than technological ones, is an all-encompassing approach to education, which, when paired with leadership support and training that is particular to roles, is the very foundation.

Despite the fact that cybersecurity training is a vital component of organisational security strategy, there is evidence to show that traditional technical security training frequently fails to accomplish the results that were intended for it. Organisations continue to encounter high rates of security events due to human error, poor retention of security-related information, and disengagement from security training programmes. This is the case despite the substantial expenditures that have been made in security education. There are several factors that contribute to the failure of security training, including an excessive dependence on rote learning, inefficient compliance-driven techniques, and security fatigue. These factors all work together to hinder long-term security awareness and shifts in behaviour.

A training approach that is extensively utilised but has been heavily criticised for its lack of effectiveness is called "rote learning." Rote learning is the process of memorising security regulations, password requirements, and procedural checklists. The development of abilities in critical thinking and decision-making is not given the same level of importance as the repeating of information in this course of action. It has been established via research in the field of educational psychology that passive learning procedures, such as memorisation and multiple-choice examinations, lead to low retention rates and limited applicability in real-world circumstances (Brown et al., 2014).

The problems of compliance-driven training further compound the ineffectiveness of traditional security education. Conventional security education is ineffectual. Regulatory frameworks such as the General Data Protection Regulation (GDPR), the International Organisation for Standardisation (ISO), and the National Institute of Standards and Technology (NIST) mandate that organisations undertake security awareness training. However, many businesses view this need as merely a checkbox exercise rather than a chance to create a meaningful security culture. Training that is driven by compliance often includes standardised modules, films that have been pre-recorded, and evaluations that are universally applicable. Employees are required to complete these elements in order to fulfil their legal duties. On the other hand, research suggests that such training does not necessarily result in changes in behaviour (Peterson & McCleery, 2014). It's possible for employees to finish training modules for the sole purpose of satisfying business obligations, without actually internalising the ideas that underlie the regulations. Employees continue to be victims of phishing attempts, poor password habits, and social engineering risks as a consequence of the fact that security behaviours continue to be inconsistent.

Security fatigue is another significant aspect that contributes to the reduction in the efficacy of security training. Employees experience cognitive overload and disengagement as a result of the excessive deployment of security measures that are not only restricted but also punishing and repetitious. According to Reeves et al. (2021), security fatigue happens when individuals get overwhelmed by the number of security demands imposed upon them. This condition causes individuals to disregard warnings, circumvent security policies, or display riskier behaviours out of irritation. Employees may attempt ways to circumvent security procedures, such as reusing passwords or deactivating security notifications, despite the fact that these measures are designed to increase security. This can lead to resistance, which is a paradoxical outcome.

The failure of security training ultimately occurs when it is preoccupied with superficial compliance or rote learning at the expense of techniques that are rich in context and experience learning. Rethinking educational design in order to emphasise interactive activities, situational learning, and long-term engagement tactics. This is necessary in order to address the gap that has been identified.

Rather than focussing on superficial rule compliance, a new approach to security education places more of an emphasis on more in-depth and long-lasting learning experiences. Studies conducted in the field of cognitive psychology have demonstrated that techniques such as scenario-based training, active learning, and spaced repetition are effective in greatly enhancing the development and retention of memories.

According to Cepeda et al. (2006), the spacing effect improves long-term memory when students revisit important topics as the intervals between their previous experiences increase. Active learning, in which participants participate actively by solving problems and discussing scenarios, helps individuals digest knowledge more efficiently than passive approaches such as reading or listening to lectures (Freeman, 2014). Active learning is a style of learning in which participants engage immediately with the material. Additionally, learners are able to practise effective answers to real-world issues through the use of simulation-based training, which helps to promote improved situational awareness when such challenges are encountered (Elendu et al., 2024).

The importance of both cognitive and emotional involvement cannot be overstated. Embedding security lessons inside tales that stimulate inquiry and empathy may be accomplished through the use of storytelling, for example (Habermas, 2018; Haven, 2007). According to Hamari et al. (2014), the use of gamification techniques, such as point scoring, leaderboards, or unlocking accomplishments, has the potential to increase motivation and decrease the monotony that is typically associated with standard procedures for security training.

These techniques are grounded in a number of different psychological theories. The theory of constructivist learning, which has its origins in the research conducted by Piaget and Vygotsky, proposes that the most efficient way for students to create knowledge is by working through issues and reflecting on their experiences (Piaget, 1972; Vygotsky, 1978). Individuals are able to internalise fundamental ideas rather than only memorising them on a surface level when they actively develop different solutions.

Bandura's Social Learning Theory emphasises the impact that observing peers and role models may have on a person's development of new behaviours (Bandura, 1977). Incorporating security champions into departments is a good example of this notion since it encourages employees to model their own behaviour after the secure procedures that are displayed by educated peers. When these champions adhere to stringent password management practices or promptly report phishing attempts, it is more likely that others will follow in their footsteps and adopt similar proactive habits.

Behavioural Conditioning, which was developed by B. F. Skinner in 1953, places an emphasis on the significance of incentives and consequences in the formulation of habits. Not only may some activities be discouraged through the use of punitive measures, but acknowledgement and positive reinforcement frequently result in more long-lasting changes in behaviour. In security environments, rewarding teams or people that spot risks immediately or follow best practices can encourage widespread adoption of protective behaviours. This can be accomplished by providing incentives. Through the incorporation of various cognitive and educational ideas, such as emotionally resonant approaches, spaced repetition, and the concepts of constructivist, social, and behavioural conditioning, security training has the potential to develop into an immersive, learner-centred practice. This change converts security education from a rote exercise into a dynamic process of discovery, reflection, and reinforcement. As a result, employee engagement is increased, and the long-term risk of the organisation is greatly reduced.

In the same way that other behaviours are most successful when they become habitual and firmly established in everyday routines, security behaviours are most effective when they become automatic. The development of security habits occurs when individuals frequently engage in secure behaviours until they become automatic. Consistent repetition of particular tasks, in conjunction with instant feedback, has been shown to be more efficient in the development of habitual behaviours than sporadic training sessions, according to research conducted in the field of behavioural psychology (Lally et al., 2010). It is possible to gradually change isolated behaviours into established habits within the field of cybersecurity by urging users to check the validity of the sender of their emails or to lock their displays whenever they leave their workstation. These acts can be further strengthened via the use of reinforcement through positive feedback, such as praise, acknowledgement, or minor rewards. On the other hand, punitive tactics run the potential of fostering fear or avoidance rather than sustainable security habits (Skinner, 1953).

The Behaviour Model constructed by BJ Fogg offers a succinct framework for comprehending the reasons behind the adoption or non-adoption of safe habits by individuals. According to Fogg (2009), the concept proposes that conduct is the result of the convergence of three components: motivation, ability, and "prompts" for the activity. Learners are guided to take suitable actions at the appropriate time by prompts, which can be notifications, gentle reminders, or triggers. For example, learners may be prompted to check external email sources or the information technology department to report suspicious behaviours. Behaviours that are considered secure have a tendency to become effortless and habitual when the level of motivation is great, the ability is straightforward, and prompts arrive frequently.

These habits are further cemented by the use of approaches that involve long-term reinforcement, which reduces the need on willpower or periodic training alone. Habit stacking, for example, is the practice of attaching a new secure activity to an existing habit that has been developed for a considerable amount of time (Clear, 2018). Employees who are accustomed to checking their calendars at the beginning of the workday might incorporate security into their normal daily routine by attaching a brief antivirus scan check to their routine. The implementation of nudging strategies, which are founded on the ideas of behavioural economics proposed by Thaler and Sunstein (2008), involves making minor design decisions that direct individuals towards behaviours that are more secure.

However, rather than depending on compliance-based techniques that require continual enforcement, the future of security education rests in the creation of behavioural interventions that integrate security into daily activities in a seamless manner. The transition from reactive security policies to proactive, entrenched security behaviours is something that may be accomplished by organisations through the utilisation of habit formation concepts, personalised reinforcement mechanisms, and adaptive training programmes. Rather than simply providing personnel with training in security awareness, the objective is to foster an atmosphere in which secure behaviours become second nature. This will ensure that the organisation is resilient over the long run against emerging security dangers.

To summarise, security education is a crucial component for modern organisations, as human error continues to be the primary factor in the occurrence of security breaches. In spite of the fact that firewalls and other technical defences are essential, they are ineffectual in the absence of a knowledgeable workforce. Because of its dependence on rote learning, compliance-driven models, and security fatigue, traditional security training frequently fails, which results in disengagement and dangerous behaviours.

Spaced repetition, scenario-based training, and active learning are all components that are included into a behavioural science-based approach to security education. This technique is designed to promote retention. Engagement may be increased by the use of techniques like as storytelling, gamification, and simulations of the real world. Additionally, psychological theories such as constructivist learning, social learning, and behavioural conditioning can be utilised to mould behaviour over the long term. The Behaviour Model developed by BJ Fogg emphasises the significance of motivation, ability, and prompts in the process of forming security habits. These habits are often reinforced via the use of habit stacking, nudging, and personalised interventions.

It is necessary for organisations to go from reactive policies to proactive, established habits in order to guarantee that security behaviours become almost second nature. The education of security personnel need to be flexible, interesting, and easily incorporated into the routines of everyday operations. Businesses have the ability to cultivate a resilient workforce that is capable of minimising the effects of changing cyber threats if they integrate security-conscious behaviours into the culture of the organisation.

REFERENCES

Bandura, A. (1977). *Social learning theory*. Prentice-Hall.
Brown, P. C., Roediger, H. L., & McDaniel, M. A. (2014). *Make it stick: The science of successful learning*. The Belknap Press of Harvard University Press.
Cepeda, N. J., Pashler, H., Vul, E., Wixted, J. T., & Rohrer, D. (2006). Distributed practice in verbal recall tasks: A review and quantitative synthesis. *Psychological Bulletin, 132*(3), 354–380.
Clear, J. (2018). *Atomic habits: An easy & proven way to build good habits & break bad ones*. Penguin Publishing Group.
Dimitrov, W. (2020). The impact of the advanced technologies over the cyber attacks surface. In R. Silhavy (Ed.), *Artificial intelligence and bioinspired computational methods*. CSOC 2020. Advances in Intelligent Systems and Computing (Vol. 1225). Springer.
Elendu, C., Amaechi, D. C., Okatta, A. U., Amaechi, E. C., Elendu, T. C., Ezeh, C. P., & Elendu, I. D. (2024). The impact of simulation-based training in medical education: A review. *Medicine, 103*(27), 1–14.
Fogg, B. (2009). A behavior model for persuasive design. In *Proceedings of the 4th International Conference on Persuasive Technology—Persuasive'09*, Vol. 40, No. 40, pp. 1–7.
Freeman, S. (2014). Active learning increases student performance in science, engineering, and mathematics. *Proceedings of the National Academy of Sciences, 111*(23), 8410–8415.
Habermas, T. (2018). Emotion and narrative.
Hamari, J. Koivisto, J., & Sarsa, H. (2014). Does gamification work?—A literature review of empirical studies on gamification. In *47th Hawaii International Conference on System Sciences, Waikoloa, HI, USA* (pp. 3025–3034).
Haven, K. (2007). *Story proof*. Libraries Unlimited eBooks.
Hughes-Lartey, K., Li, M., Botchey, F.E. and Qin, Z. (2021). Human factor, a critical weak point in the information security of an organization's Internet of things. *Heliyon, 7*(3).
Kadena, E., & Gupi, M. (2021). Human factors in cybersecurity. *Security Science Journal, 2*(2), 51–64.

Lally, P., van Jaarsveld, C. H. M., Potts, H. W. W., & Wardle, J. (2010). How are habits formed: Modelling habit formation in the real world. *European Journal of Social Psychology, 40*(6), 998–1009.

Peterson, K., & McCleery, E. (2014). *Evidence brief: The effectiveness of mandatory computer-based trainings on government ethics, workplace harassment, or privacy and information security-related topics [Internet]*. Department of Veterans Affairs.

Piaget, J. I. (1972). Psychology and epistemology: Towards a theory of knowledge.

Reeves, A., Delfabbro, P., & Calic, D. (2021). Encouraging employee engagement with cybersecurity: How to tackle cyber fatigue. *Sage Open, 11*(1).

Sasi, T., Lashkari, A. H., Lu, R., Xiong, P., & Iqbal, S. (2023). A comprehensive survey on IoT attacks: Taxonomy, detection mechanisms and challenges. *Journal of Information and Intelligence, 2*(6).

Skinner, B. F. (1953). *Science and human behavior*. Macmillan.

Thaler, R. H., & Sunstein, C. R. (2008). *Nudge: Improving decisions about health, wealth, and happiness*. Yale University Press.

Vygotsky, L. S. (1978). Mind in society: Development of higher psychological processes. M. Cole, V. Jolm-Steiner, S. Scribner, & E. Souberman (Eds.). Harvard University Press.

Index

A
Accountability, 38, 41, 42, 44, 88
Adaptive risk management, 12, 13
Aleatory and epistemic uncertainty, 10, 13
Anchoring bias, 38, 40, 44
Attention and memory constraints, 39

B
Behavioural change, 78
Behavioural indicators, 49, 71
Behavioural risk perception, 12
Behavioural security culture, 38
Bystander effect, 41, 42, 44

C
Cognitive biases, 3, 4, 10, 11, 17, 24, 38, 57, 59, 61, 62
Cognitive load, 3, 39
Collaborative security framework, 3
Compliance, 25, 38, 42, 44, 59, 61, 78, 87, 90, 96, 98, 99
Conformity, 38, 41, 44

Crime Prevention Through Environmental Design (CPTED), 4, 74, 76, 77, 79
Criminal profiling, 48, 51–53
Criminological theories, 68, 69, 71, 73, 74
Cultural Cognition Framework, 24, 26, 30

D
Dark Triad (narcissism, psychopathy, Machiavellianism), 48
Diffusion of responsibility, 38, 40, 41, 44

E
Emotional appeals, 4, 28

F
Fear appeals, 43, 78

G
Gamification of learning, 5
Group dynamics, 38, 40, 44
Groupthink, 4, 38, 40, 41, 44

H
Heuristic errors, 40
Heuristics, 10, 13, 16, 17, 20, 38, 40, 59
Human-centric security, 3
Human vulnerabilities, 4, 49, 58, 62, 88, 90

I
Information deficit model, 3, 24, 26, 30
Insider threats, 2, 4, 42, 47–50, 52, 53, 68, 69, 75
Interdisciplinary approach, 2
International cooperation, 88, 89
ISO 31000, 11

M
Media amplification, 28
Mental Models Approach, 24, 26, 30
Message framing, 28
Misinformation, 16, 24, 28–30
Motivation, 11, 25, 38, 42–45, 48–50, 52, 53, 69–71, 73, 74, 79, 100–102
Motivation and emotions, 38, 44

O
Offender profiling, 48, 51
Optimism bias, 16, 20, 38, 40, 44
Organised crime, 4, 68

P
Personality traits in cyber/offline crime, 70
Phishing and spear phishing, 59
Profiling, 48, 49, 51, 52
Psychology-based training, 5
Public–private partnerships, 5, 86–88, 91

R
Rational Choice Theory, 4, 67–69
Risk communication, 2, 3, 16, 18–20, 23–31
Risk perception, 3, 6, 10, 12, 13, 16, 18–20, 24, 26, 40, 44
Routine Activity Theory, 4, 67–69, 75

S
Scenario-based exercises, 96, 99, 102
Security culture, 5, 20, 38, 41, 44, 86, 90, 91, 98
Situational Crime Prevention (SCP), 4, 72, 74, 75, 79
Social Amplification of Risk Framework (SARF), 19
Social engineering, 2, 4, 5, 6, 38, 40, 42, 49, 57–63, 71, 76, 86, 88, 90, 99
Social media and risk, 29
Strain Theory, 4, 6, 67–69, 71
Stress and burnout, 43
Subjective risk assessment, 16

U
Uncertainty, 3, 10, 11, 38, 40

Z
Zero-day vulnerabilities, 11, 86

The manufacturer's authorised representative in the EU is Springer Nature Customer Service Centre GmbH, Europaplatz 3, 69115 Heidelberg, Germany. If you have any concerns regarding our products, please contact ProductSafety@springernature.com

Printed and bound by CPI Group (UK) Ltd, Croydon, CR0 4YY

02/03/2026

02062925-0003